Just-Add-Kids Games for Children's Ministry

Group

Loveland, Colorado

JUST-ADD-KIDS GAMES FOR CHILDREN'S MINISTRY

Copyright © 1998 Group Publishing, Inc.

Credits

Contributing Authors: Michelle Anthony, Mikal Keefer, Kelly Martin, Marilyn Meiklejohn, Ken Niles, Dave Thornton, Lisa Dawn Tyler, Wendy Lee Watros, Becki West, Gordon D. West, and Paul Woods
Book Acquisitions Editor: Lori Haynes Niles
Development Editor: Jody Brolsma
Chief Creative Officer: Joani Schultz
Copy Editor: Debbie Gowensmith
Art Director: Jean Bruns
Cover Art Director: Jeff A. Storm
Computer Graphic Artist: Randy Kady
Cover Designer: Lisa Chandler
Illustrator: Shelley Dieterichs-Morrison
Cover Photography: Stock Imagery
Production Manager: Peggy Naylor

Library of Congress Cataloging-in-Publication Data

Just-add-kids games for children's ministry / [contributing authors,
    Michelle Anthony ... et al.].
        p. cm.
    Includes index.
    ISBN 0-7644-2112-3
    1. Games in Christian education. 2. Christian education
of children. I. Anthony, Michelle.
BV1536.3.J87 1998
259'.22--dc21   98-20200
                                                                   CIP

10 9 8 7 6 5 4 3 2 1   07 06 05 04 03 02 01 00 99 98

Printed in the United States of America.

Contents ~~~~~

FRIEND BUILDERS 51

OUTDOOR ADVENTURES 71

QUIET QUESTERS 91

Introduction

Make your classroom *the* place to be with this collection of easy-to-use and easy-to-pull-off games that require nothing more than what's at your fingertips!

You'll find games that can be adapted to almost any Bible story or lesson so that you'll never lose a lesson to drooping eyelids again.

You'll find games that help you get the wiggles under control so that you can go on with a dynamite lesson.

You'll find games that *teach* lessons in a fun and nonthreatening way.

You'll find games you can take your kids outdoors to play when you finish your lessons early.

You'll find games that help kids teach each other life lessons through developing Christ-centered relationships.

You'll find games that review previous lessons and call on kids' own Bible knowledge.

And best of all, you'll find games you can pull off on the spot because the most supplies any of them require is paper, crayons or markers, or masking tape—things you almost always have on hand. Many of them require no supplies at all—just add kids!

With the variations suggested and those you come up with on your own, you'll have hundreds of games at your disposal. You'll be a Playmaster without a lot of prior planning.

You see, one of your most important roles as a Christian educator is to make learning about Christian life fun. Play helps kids connect to important spiritual truths. And it helps kids want to come back again and again, so you have multiple opportunities to reinforce the lessons you want kids to learn most: that God loves them and wants them to be in loving relationship with him through his Son, Jesus.

So tuck these games under your belt. Keep them handy so you can use them any time and anyplace to help kids grow in their Christian faith!

BIBLE BLASTERS

Kids should have a *blast* with the Bible! The games in this section are fun and will help your kids enjoy interacting with the Bible in new and different ways. Best of all, you'll find ways to adapt these Bible Blasters to fit any story that is part of your lesson, and you'll be sure that you're helping your kids connect to God's Word in ways that beat the blahs!

Jiggly Jelly

Early elementary

Turn any Bible story into an active experience with this highly adaptable game.

Tell the kids that they are "jiggly jelly" filling a bowl. Have them all stand together in an open space and begin to wiggle like a bowl full of jelly. Tell them that a huge hand is now picking up the bowl and shaking it. Have kids shake and wiggle like they think a bowl of jelly would shake. Next tell the kids that the hand has stopped shaking the bowl, and have them slow down and stop.

Then tell kids to wiggle as you raise your hand in the air and shake it and to slow down and stop as you lower your hand.

Use this game to act out any of the following Bible stories:

The Great Flood (Genesis 7:17-24; 8:1-14)

Tell the kids that they are a bowl of jiggly jelly on Noah's breakfast table in the ark! Have the kids jiggle like a bowl of jelly as you tell the story of the great flood. Include the water rising from still, small puddles to gently rocking lakes to wildly flowing streams and rivers and finally to a raging, tossing ocean that covers the entire earth for 150 days. Continue the story as the winds blow the waters, the storm stops, and the water recedes.

Moses Parts the Red Sea (Exodus 14:10-31)

Paraphrase this story, and have the kids be a bowl of jiggly jelly that a small boy has packed away in his knapsack as he runs for safety with his family. Have the kids jiggle as the Israelites walk across the desert to reach the Red Sea, as they run across the dry ground after Moses parts the water, as they run faster because the Egyptian soldiers are pursuing them, and as they stop to watch the Red Sea fall back on the Egyptians.

Jesus Calms the Storm (Luke 8:22-25)

Have the kids pretend to be a bowl of jiggly jelly that one of the disciples packed for a snack. As you tell the story, encourage kids to act out what the jiggly jelly would have done as the disciples set out on the boat, then as it began to rain and the boat gently rocked, then as the storm raged, and finally as the boat stopped rocking after Jesus calmed the storm.

After the Bible story, gather the kids together and talk about how they would have felt if they had been in the storm and had seen Jesus calm it.

PLAYMASTER'S POINTERS

Be creative! Whenever your Bible story has great movement, you can plug in this activity to help kinesthetic learners tune in to your lesson.

Mime the Message

BEST FOR All ages

Whether you are teaching or reviewing a specific Bible story or a biblical concept, have the kids explore it by using this group twist on the classic pantomime.

PLAYMASTER'S POINTERS

If you don't have a specific Scripture passage in mind, here are some sure winners:
● the good shepherd (Psalm 23 and John 10:1-15)
● the parable of the sower (Matthew 13:1-9; 18-23)
● the parable of the prodigal son (Luke 15:11-32)

Say: **Everyone is going to get a chance to be an actor in today's Bible story. But it's a silent story, so you will be mimes rather than speaking actors. In a moment I'll ask all of you to stand at the back wall and face the wall so you can't see the front of the room. One at a time, I'll ask you to turn around and face the front. You will get a "private" showing of today's Bible story. Then you'll join the** mime troupe. You'll act out the same story, or what you believe to be the story, for the next person. If you think you have something new to add that will help the next person identify the story, add it. Otherwise—or if you don't know the story—do exactly what the other person is already doing so you're acting together.

After the last person watches the story being mimed, he or she will guess the story or message. If he or she can't guess it, you'll all have a chance to guess, so don't give away your ideas!

Choose one person to be the first mime, and have the rest of the children stand at the back wall. Tell the mime the story or message you have chosen. Help the child develop a pantomime if necessary. In random order, call the children who are standing against the wall so none of them have to wait longer than their individual ability allows. Encourage all the children to continue to pantomime

This activity as described is best for smaller classes.

If you have a larger class, have kids form smaller groups in different parts of the room. For even more fun, break the story into different segments, and have each group act out part of the story. Have the last performers of each group link the whole story together to see if anyone can get the "big picture" from this final performance.

until the last child has been called and to remember the rule of silent activity throughout the game. Allow the last child two chances to guess the Bible story, and then open it up to the mime troupe for guesses. Let the kids discuss the "giveaway clues" in the pantomime as a way to open up the main points of the Bible story or message. Ask:

- **What were the giveaway clues in this mime?**
- **How did you *know* what story was being mimed?**

The Master Potter

 All ages

Help visual, auditory, and kinesthetic learners act out the Bible story in this real hands-on game.

Select one person who will serve as the model. Give the model a slip of paper that tells him or her to pose to represent a significant event in the life of a Bible character. Include a few Bible references for the event. Allow a few minutes for the model to think about how to represent the event while you explain the rules to the rest of the class.

If you have not already selected a story, here are some "works of art" to help you get started with this game:

- Simon of Cyrene carrying Jesus' cross (Luke 23:26)
- Moses stretching out his hand to part the Red Sea (Exodus 14:16, 21-22)
- Jesus praying in the Garden of Gethsemane (Mark 14:32-36)

Have the other kids form pairs. One member of each pair will be the "clay" while the other will be the "artist." Say: **In just a moment, our model will strike a pose for all of you artists. It is your job to re-create the model's pose with your clay.**

When I say "go," all of you who are clay must close your eyes and keep them closed. Only the artists should see the model. Clay, you must listen and follow the instructions from your artists. You may not open your eyes until I tell you to do so!

Those of you who are artists must give your clay the best instructions you can *without touching the clay.*

Signal the clay to close their eyes and the model to

strike his or her pose. Then give the artists and clay a brief time to work. Before you allow the clay to open their eyes, have the model stop posing.

Say: **Clay, stay in position and open your eyes to see what each artist has created. Raise your hand when you are ready to guess what Bible event we were re-creating.**

If no one comes up with the right answer, have the model tell what Bible reference was written on his or her slip of paper. Have each of the clay/artist pairs look up the passage and discover what event they have just artistically represented!

Instead of having the artists tell the clay what to do, have the artists silently mold the clay into the form the model is demonstrating.

Just One More Thing...

Grades 2-5

Use this verbal game to provide kids with a quiet but fun Bible story review.

To start, have kids form a circle sitting on the floor or in chairs. Say: **Raise your hand if you remember a Bible character's name from one of our recent lessons.** Pause. **Put your hands down. Now raise your hand if you remember a story about one of the Bible characters we've learned about.** Pause. **We're going to play a game that needs your creative juices and an active memory.**

This game is called Just One More Thing..., and here's how you play. I'll start by saying the name of a Bible character. Then I'll point to someone, signaling him or her to add a word that helps create a sentence about that character. We'll continue around the circle to the right with each person adding one word to make our sentence as long—and as true—as possible. If it's your turn and you think it's time to end the sentence, call out "period." Then the next person in the circle will name a different Bible character and we'll go again, making one long sentence. Here's an example:

If I say "Noah," you might help build a sentence by saying

(point to a different child as you say each word), **"built a very, very large boat called an ark because God told him to build it for all the animals in the world like the lion."**

Of course, we can make our sentence as long as we like, naming all the animals we can think up. The longer the sentence, the greater our fun and the better our review.

Begin by calling out a Bible character's name and pointing to the first student to add the next word. Call "time" when each sentence has provided a good review of previous material, or wait for a player to call "period!" When the end of the sentence is called, the next person in line must introduce a different Bible character's name from a recent lesson. Continue as long as the game provides a strong review for previous lessons.

Arky, Arky

All ages

Get all the "animals" into the "ark" with this mind-bending action game.

Show the kids these motions, which they'll use to play a game:
- Bird—place thumbs under arms and flap twice.
- Fish—place palms together and make a swimming motion with hands.
- Mammal—use one hand to fan face, to demonstrate that you are warmblooded as all mammals are.
- Reptile—move one arm to make an "s."

Designate an area to be the "ark." Have children form two equal teams and line up along two opposite walls. Stand in the center of the room, and instruct the first person in each line to run to you. Have those two children count to three together. On three, have both children simultaneously make one of the four signs. If the signs match, have children quickly proceed to the ark. If the signs don't match, children must run back to their lines, tag the next people, and go to the ends of their lines. If the first two players get to go to the ark, the second two players may run to you as soon as the first two reach the ark.

Play until everyone is in the ark. End with the rousing celebration song "Arky, Arky."

Tower of Babbling

Upper elementary

BEST FOR

Explore the value of clear communication in this game that's based on the story of the tower of Babel.

Have kids form trios. Announce that in a few moments, you'll give each trio ten crayons, several feet of tape, and three sheets of paper. Each trio's job is to use those supplies to build the tallest, sturdiest tower it can make.

Say: **In your trios, take a minute to discuss how you'll make a tower with those supplies. I'll drift around to hear what you're planning.**

After about a minute, announce these two rules:

1. Everyone must participate. You've got to work together to build your tower. No watchers—everyone is a helper!

2. Each person in your group can say one word only. The person wearing the most red can only say "booga-booga." The person to the right of the "booga-booga" person can only say "oops." And the third person can only say "yowza." Let's all practice our special languages. Let kids practice out loud, and then distribute the supplies. Say: **OK, you have four minutes to build your towers!**

Wander around, encouraging all the children to participate.

Give two- and one-minute warnings. When time has passed, ask children to show off their creations. Praise all efforts. Gather children around you, and ask:

● **Was it easy or difficult to build your towers? Why?**

● **What would have made it easier for you to work as a team?**

Say: **When I was watching you work, I was reminded of a passage in the book of Genesis.** Read aloud Genesis 11: 1-9. Ask:

● **Why do you think God didn't want this group of people to work well together?** (See verse 4.)

● **How was your experience building your towers like or unlike what happened to the people building the tower in this story?**

● **If God kept people from accomplishing a wrong goal by confusing their communication, what might be important to remember when you are trying to accomplish a right goal?**

Say: **God seemed to show these people that their desire for greatness was way out of line. By confusing their language, he kept them from accomplishing their plans. God knew how important communication was to accomplishing any goal. Maybe the most important part of the lesson for us to remember is that our ability to communicate is a gift from God and that we need to use it to honor him.**

Salt Statues

 All ages

Kids must overcome distractions in this no-peeking game.

Say: In Genesis, God tells a story about a city full of wicked people. They made God very angry, so he decided to destroy the city. But in this same city lived a man named Lot and his family, who God loved very much. God decided he would allow Lot and his family to live if they left the wicked city, but God warned them not to look back. Lot's wife missed her home and looked back. She turned into a statue of salt because she didn't obey God's command (Genesis 19:12-17, 26).

Have the kids stand, spacing themselves around the room. Say: **I will tell you some things to do. You must carry out each direction without looking at me no matter how curious you are about what I'm doing. If you look back, I will call your name, and you will become a pillar of salt that is frozen in position like Lot's wife when she looked back. Everybody ready?**

Give the students some simple things to do such as telling others their favorite color or finding someone with the same type of shoes. Every time you mention a new task, any "pillars of salt" may "unfreeze" and start over. Try to entice the students to look at you by moving about or singing silly songs or making strange noises. After several rounds, gather the children, and ask:

● **What made this game difficult?**

Say: **Sometimes things distract us from obeying God. That was Lot's wife's problem. She was distracted by other things and was careless about following God's commands.** Ask:

● **What are some things that distract you from obeying God?**

Say: **We can miss out on things God wants us to enjoy just as Lot's wife missed out on God's gifts for her.** Play several more rounds just for fun. Challenge the children to beat their own record of "not looking back."

Enlist one or more fellow "distracters" from among the players by arming them with salt shakers to shake noisily. These distracters also can call out a name if a player looks at him or her. This makes the game even more challenging!

On the Shore; Cross the Sea

BEST FOR **All ages**

Challenge your kids' listening skills with this fast-paced jumping game.

Use masking tape to mark a line on the floor in the middle of your classroom. Say: **As the Israelites stood on the shore of the Red Sea, they had a choice to make. Would they obey God and cross the sea, or would they stand on the shore and**

Play this game with these other Bible stories:

● crossing into Canaan (Say, "Take the land" or "Desert sand.")

● David and Jonathan (Say, "Arrows here" or "Arrows beyond.")

● Peter heals the crippled beggar (Say, "Silver and gold" or "Rise up and walk.")

wait for the Egyptians to come? Today we're going to play a game that reminds us of this Bible story. The line on the floor marks the boundary between the sea and the shore. Everyone should stand on the left side of the line now, and we'll call this the shore. When I say, "Cross the sea," everyone should jump to the other side. When I say, "On the shore," everyone should jump back to the left side. Pay close attention because just as in the game Simon Says, you jump over the line only when I say the phrases exactly the way I just said them. That's "On the shore" and "Cross the sea."

As you play this game, keep the kids on their toes by using phrases such as "In the shore," "On the sea," "Out to sea," or "Come to shore." Vary the pace and volume of your instructions for fun.

Moses and the Fiery Serpents

BEST FOR All ages

Play this game in conjunction with the story of the bronze snake found in Numbers 21:4-9.

Play this game in a large, cleared, indoor area. Have all the players remove their shoes. Choose a "Moses" to stand in a designated safe zone at one end of the playing area. Choose two players (or more if your group is large) to be the "fiery serpents." The rest of the class are the "children of Israel."

The game starts with everyone lying down. The fiery serpents slither on their bellies among the children of Israel. (The serpents must keep their tummies on the floor; they cannot be on their hands and knees.) When Moses calls, "Fiery serpents!" the children of Israel jump up and try to run to the safe zone while avoiding being tagged by a serpent. When a child is tagged, he or she must quickly drop to the floor and then join the serpents in trying to tag others.

Fiery serpents may not enter the safe zone, and the children of

Israel who enter must go out to rescue others by touching any serpent on the ankle. The healed serpent and the rescuer hold hands and return to the safe zone. They then must go out to rescue others.

The rescuers may be touched and turned into serpents while going out but not while returning with a "healed" serpent.

The game continues until all are saved or all become serpents.

Morning Manna

Early and middle elementary

Help kids remember the story of God providing manna for the people of Israel, and encourage kids to be helpful to each other.

Give each child a sheet of paper. Have each person tear his or her sheet into twelve relatively equal pieces. While kids are tearing, use masking tape to make a line about three feet from one end of the room, parallel to that wall. Then gather all the pieces of paper, and have kids stand behind the line. Say: **We're going to pretend these little pieces of paper are manna as the Bible describes in Exodus 16:14-16. During the Israelites' years in the desert, each morning when they woke up, manna would be all over the ground. They would gather the manna and use it for food. But each family was to gather only enough for that day.**

When I say, "It's nighttime," you'll close your eyes, and I'll scatter the manna around the room. Then I'll shout, "Rise and shine!" and you'll all rush out to gather your manna. The goal of this game is for each person to gather exactly twelve pieces of manna and to get back across the line. I'll keep time, and we'll see how fast everyone can get back behind the line with twelve pieces of manna.

Declare it nighttime, have kids close their eyes, and scatter the manna around the room. Then shout: **Rise and shine!** and start timing.

If some kids get twelve pieces of manna and return quickly, remind kids that the time runs until everyone has twelve pieces of manna and is back across the line. Ask kids if they can think of a way to make that happen faster.

When everyone is back across the line, tell kids how long they took. Then ask:

● **How do you think we can cut our time?**

Collect the manna, and repeat the game a couple of times, encouraging kids to improve their time by helping each other get the right amount of manna quickly.

Crossing Over Jordan

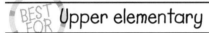 **Upper elementary**

Overcoming obstacles has never been this much fun!

Say: **The people of Israel were slaves in Egypt for many years. God sent Moses to lead them out of Egypt and take them to the Promised Land. But when they had escaped from the Egyptian army and Pharaoh, God caused the Israelites to wander in the wilderness for forty years so they would learn to trust and worship only him.**

The Bible tells us that this was not a very happy time for the people of Israel. They had many obstacles to overcome during their time of wandering. This game will help us imagine what it was like for the Israelites finally to cross the Jordan River and enter into the Promised Land of Canaan.

Divide the room into two territories with an imaginary Jordan River in between. Explain to the children that they are the people of Israel and that everyone must get across the river in order to enter the Promised Land.

As one last reminder that the Israelites faced many obstacles in the desert and needed to learn to work together in the Promised Land, they will create a human bridge across the Jordan River, which God cleared for the Israelites to walk across. A human bridge is an obstacle course made by everyone in the group. One by one, each player adds to the bridge, standing or crouching in position. Each player must climb over or crawl under the players who are already part of the bridge. For example, the first player stands with his or her legs apart. The second player crawls under the first player and then crouches in a ball. The third player crawls under the first player and over the second player and ends up as a tunnel on all fours. Each player may choose any position. Players may consider holding arms in hoops for others to step through or lying on the floor for others to step over.

When the last player is added to the bridge, the first player must go through the whole course and assume a position at the end. Continue until all of the people of Israel have safely moved to the other side of the Jordan River and have entered the Promised Land.

Have the kids form equal teams to have a relay. Make it more challenging by adding the rule that no person can assume the same position more than once.

Samuel Listened Like This

BEST FOR **Middle and upper elementary**

Could Samuel have gotten the wiggles while waiting for the Lord? Who knows?

Say: **When Samuel was a small boy, he was taken to the temple to live with Eli the priest. One night after Samuel had gone to sleep, he heard a voice calling, "Samuel! Samuel!"**

Samuel jumped up and ran to Eli, saying, "Here I am. What do you need?" But Eli said, "I didn't call you. Go back to bed."

This happened three times, and finally Eli realized that the Lord was calling Samuel. He said to the boy, "Go back to bed, and if someone calls again, say, 'Lord, your servant is listening.'" So Samuel went back to bed and listened. I wonder if he was absolutely still while he was listening. Maybe he wiggled a little. There are so many ways to wiggle. Let's think of some for this game.

Have the children stand in a circle. Choose one player to be the leader. The leader begins by saying, "Samuel listened to the Lord."

Then the rest of the group answers, "How did Samuel listen to the Lord?" The leader then says, "Samuel listened like this, like this" and repeats a small gesture such as shaking his or her head or bending and unbending one finger. The rest of the group mimics the gesture and answers, "Like this, like this."

Everyone in the group continues to repeat the gesture as the next player in line says, "Samuel listened to the Lord"; then the others respond as before: "How did Samuel listen to the Lord?" The second player adds another gesture to the first so that everyone is making two movements at the same time.

The game continues around the circle, with each player adding a gesture. Each added gesture makes the combination of movements more difficult as well as more fun. You probably will not get all the way around the circle before everyone is laughing too hard to continue. At this point, stop the action and begin again with the next person in the circle becoming the new leader. Continue until everyone has had a turn to add a new gesture.

The game works best if you start off with small gestures with fingers and noses and work up to the bigger things like arms and legs.

Use this game as a "wiggle tamer" when you're telling a story, substituting "I can listen to the Lord like this, like this."

Jonah Jump

BEST FOR Early elementary

Cast lots to discover who is causing such a raging sea.

You'll need a sheet of newsprint or a large piece of construction paper for half of the kids. Also cut enough small pieces of paper for half the kids to have one, and mark one piece with an X. Set these aside.

Have one half of the group form a ship in any way they want and the other half stand around the outside of the ship. Give each of the outer children a large sheet of paper to hold by the edges.

Say: **God told Jonah to go to Nineveh and preach to try to get the people to turn from their wickedness. But Jonah didn't obey. Instead he got on a ship and went in the opposite direction.**

God sent a storm. Direct the children on the outside of the ship to start shaking their papers to make a storm sound. **The crew was really afraid because there was nothing they could do to save the ship. So they cast lots to find out who caused the storm.** Have each child in the ship pick one of the small pieces of paper from your cupped hands or whatever is available in the classroom. The child who chooses the piece of paper with the X is "Jonah." **When the lot fell on Jonah, they knew he was responsible for the storm. Jonah told them the storm would stop if they threw him into the sea.**

Have the "crew" then put Jonah outside the ship while singing the following song to the tune of the chorus of "Jesus Loves Me."

> **Out! Out goes Jonah!**
> **Out! Out goes Jonah!**
> **Out! Out goes Jonah**
> **So God will calm this storm.**

Have the children on the outside of the ship "swallow up" Jonah. Then have Jonah take a sheet of paper from one of the other children, and have that child take his or her place in the ship. The original Jonah becomes part of the storm. Play as long as kids are interested.

Whale Ate Jonah

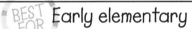 **Early elementary**

Let kids have fun as they remember what happened to Jonah.

Have children play the following variation of "London Bridge." During the first verse of the following song, have two kids form the whale by holding each other's hands high in the air. Have the other children pass under the arms of the "whale," marching around and singing the song until the sentence "A whale ate Jonah." At that sentence, have the whale drop its arms and capture one of the children as "Jonah."

During the second verse, have the whale shake Jonah around as Jonah prays with folded hands. On the last sentence of the second verse, "God spared Jonah," have the whale release Jonah.

During the third verse, have Jonah stand in the center and shake his or her index finger at the other children as they march around him. For the last phrase, have kids shout, "and God saved them!" Then have everyone stop and raise an index finger high in the air in celebration of God saving the Ninevites.

> **Jonah ran away from God** *(kids march in a circle under the whale's arms),*
> **Away from God,**
> **Away from God.**
> **Jonah ran away from God.**
> **A whale ate Jonah.** *(Whale captures Jonah.)*
>
> **Jonah prayed inside the whale** *(whale shakes Jonah as he or she prays),*
> **Inside the whale,**
> **Inside the whale.**
> **Jonah prayed inside the whale.**
> **God spared Jonah.** *(Whale releases Jonah.)*
>
> **Jonah preached to the Ninevites** *(kids circle Jonah as he or she preaches),*
> **The Ninevites,**
> **The Ninevites.**
> **Jonah preached to the Ninevites,**
> **And God saved them.** *(Kids raise index fingers in the air and shout.)*

Play the game several times, allowing different kids to be the whale and Jonah.

Building Buddies

BEST FOR Early elementary

Help children understand the value of a solid faith foundation through this fun action game.

S ay: **When Jesus taught about the wise and foolish builders** (Matthew 7:24-27), **he was talking about building our lives on a solid foundation. That solid foundation is faith in** Jesus Christ. **When our lives are built on faith in Jesus, we'll be able to stand firm against the troubles we face. But if our lives are built on a weak foundation, we may fail when troubles come. Let's see what it's like to have a solid foundation.**

Have kids form three groups. Have one group be the "wise" group, another be the "foolish" group, and the third be the "wind and flood" group.

Have kids in the wise and foolish groups get on their hands and knees, a few feet apart. Instruct the wise group members to position themselves with their hands and knees spread wide. Tell the foolish group members to position themselves with their hands and knees close together. Then say: **You're all houses. Let's see what difference your foundation makes when the wind and flood come. You may not change the position of your hands and knees when the storm comes.**

If one group needs to be smaller than the others, make the smaller group the wind and flood group.

Have the wind and flood group begin making storm noises and go around the room trying to push kids over by putting their right thumbs on top of their left thumbs and pushing with their palms. After all the foolish group members are pushed over, stop the game, have groups change roles, and play the game again. Play the game a third time so all kids have a chance to play all roles. Then gather the kids, and let them talk about what they learned from this game. Ask:

● **What are some things that feel like storms in your life?**

● **What are some things you can do to build a firm foundation so that those things won't "blow you over"?**

Say: **God wants us to trust Jesus as our faith foundation so that when those stormy times come, we can stay upright just as those who had a firm foundation did when we played our game.**

Shoe Fishing

All ages

Encourage kids to remember that God sometimes provides for our needs in unexpected ways.

Say: **In Matthew 17, we find the story of the disciples and Jesus coming to a town and needing to pay taxes. Not having the money, Peter got worried. Jesus told Peter to go fishing. Peter must have thought, "Jesus, at a time like this?" But when Peter obeyed God, he found the money he needed right in the mouth of the fish!**

Have the children form two or more teams of no more than eight. Have all the children take off their shoes and put them on a designated table which will serve as the lake. You will need to randomly place small wads of paper in about half of the shoes to represent coins. Don't let anyone see which shoes contain the "coins"! Next have kids stand about fifteen feet away from the lake and run relay-style to "go fish" for their two shoes. When kids find their shoes, they may keep any shoe that has a coin in it. Those that don't have coins need to be "thrown back" into the lake. After everyone has finished, count the "coins" from each team.

TRY THIS

Let the kids trade in their coins for chocolate "coins" for each team member to remind kids that God always provides for us—sometimes in unexpected ways.

Talent in Many Colors

Upper elementary

Use this quiet game to encourage children to do the best they can with what they have.

Have the kids sit around a table, and distribute one piece of paper to each child. Give a crayon to each child, making sure that no two children get the same color and that brown, black, and gray are included in the group. Explain that students will have five minutes to create the most original and well-developed pictures they can with the colors they have been given. Explain that after each minute, they'll be instructed to pass the paper they're drawing on to the student to their left without discussion and continue drawing on the paper they receive.

When the papers are back to their original owners, read the story of the talents found in Matthew 25:14-30. Ask:

● **What do you think was the best contribution you were able to make to a picture?**

● **Did the color you were given automatically determine the value of what you were able to add to a picture?**

● **Did those of you who were limited by dull colors feel frustration, or were you able to use these colors to the contribute something valuable? How?**

Remind the children of the story of the talents. Ask the children to compare the game to the Bible story. Ask:

● **What made the biggest difference in what a person was able to contribute to a picture: the color or how the color was used? Why?**

● **What does that show you about the gifts and talents you have been given?**

Say: **God has given each of us unique talents. Not everyone's talent looks neon bright. Some of our talents may seem pretty dull and ordinary. But if we use our talents wisely, God will honor each effort.**

Paralytic Pals

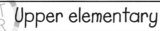

BEST FOR **Upper elementary**

Help kids understand the efforts that the paralyzed man's friends made to bring him to Jesus for healing.

Have the kids form teams of five (or more if your class is not divisible by five). Explain that kids will be running a relay race to get a friend to Jesus just as some men took their friend to Jesus in Mark 2:1-5. As in the Bible story, kids will have four team members help a fifth person get to "Jesus" at the end of the playing area. Have each "paralytic" sit in a chair. Each member of the teams must take part in transporting the paralytics.

When a team safely arrives at the person who plays Jesus, the paralytic is "healed" and remains with Jesus while the other four players run with the chair back to the starting line. Then the action repeats with a different paralytic selected by the team.

As fewer and fewer friends are available to help, each transport gets a little bit harder. Finally one player is left to transport the last paralytic.

Tell kids they need to think through who these last two players will be. They'll need a bigger, stronger player to be the friend for a smaller, lighter paralytic. The first team to get everyone to Jesus yells out, "We have never seen anything like this!" (Mark 2:12) and runs back to the starting line, where they can be seated and cheer the rest of the teams on.

PLAYMASTER'S POINTERS

Depending on your play area, it may be wise to turn the chair so that the back drags on the ground rather than the legs. The paralytic can sit knees-to-chin to fit on the chair back.

Magnifying Glass

BEST FOR Early elementary

Practice the art of careful observation of both physical and spiritual realities!

This game is played by letting one child silently select an object that's clearly in view and then identify it to the other children by color only. The rest of the children try to guess the object by this clue only. The child who guesses correctly chooses the next object but identifies it only by its shape.

Allow each child a turn, but change the clue category each time a child chooses a new object. Try these categories: estimated weight, texture, temperature, purpose, or the sound it makes. Play until every child has had a turn selecting an object.

Read aloud John 1:10-12, and ask:

● **Why didn't the people around Jesus know he was God's Son?**

● **What do you think people expected when they were looking for God's Son?**

● **What kinds of things can you look for when you are trying to see Jesus or his love in your life?**

Say: **Our game helped us to be observant about the things around us. We probably would get better with practice. We need to practice looking for Jesus' love in our lives, too, even though we can't see him with our eyes.**

TRY THIS

Ask children to close their eyes; then give children a clue about an object they saw in the room before they closed their eyes, and have them try to guess the object.

One Body, Many Parts

BEST FOR Upper elementary

Practice working together toward one goal as the early church learned to do.

Have each student choose a partner, and provide each pair with a sheet of newsprint and a crayon or marker. Allow each pair a minute or two to decide on a scene from a recently studied Bible story. Once a pair has decided on a scene, tell partners they may no longer speak to each other. Have each pair work together by holding the same crayon or marker to draw its scene. Limit the drawing time to five minutes.

Once the students are finished with their pictures, tape or tack them on the wall, and gather the students together. Read aloud 1 Corinthians 12:12-31. Ask the students to share their feelings about the game.

● **How was it to work together without words?**

● **How did each member of the pair work together as one body with many parts?**

Point out that there was more at work than just two hands. There were also two minds thinking, two personalities, and lots of legs and arms to maneuver around! Ask:

● **How does this remind you of this class or of life in general?**

● **What can this game help you remember about working together?**

Emphasize how each member of the pair had valuable

contributions to make and how success involved both leading and following, each at the right time.

Doubt Ball

Upper elementary

Give kids a chance to see and experience what happens to one who doubts.

Play this game in a gym or other large, cleared area. Mark off a line about three feet from each of two opposing walls. Have the kids form groups of four, and gather them in the center of the playing area. Each group will need one piece of paper wadded into a ball. In each group, have kids form pairs that will work together.

Read aloud James 1:5-6. Say: **In each of your groups, two of you will try to blow the paper ball over one line, and two of you will try to blow the ball over the other line. Throughout your attempt, each of you will have to maintain your position in relation to the ball.** Direct the kids to lie on their tummies on four sides of the paper ball. Give a signal, and have the kids begin. After about five minutes, call time. Ask:
- **How difficult was it to get your ball across the line?**
- **What caused you to have trouble?**
- **What would this activity tell you if we said that wisdom was the reward for getting the ball across the line, and your opponents represented doubt?**
- **What if you had no opponents?**
- **What if you have no doubt when you ask God for wisdom?**

Say: **God always wants us to have his wisdom. We need to trust him to give it to us and not let doubts distract us.**

ENERGY BOOMERS

Use Energy Boomers when you want to give your kids an opportunity for extraordinary fun. You'll find ways to tame the wiggles, run off the jiggles, and take advantage of the squirms! Some games are Bible-based; others are purely for fun. Play these games in tight spaces, big gyms, or the great outdoors, and then get back to your regularly scheduled programming.

Pencil Point

All ages

Kids have fun while beating the wiggles in this quick circle relay that gives them a break when they need it.

Have kids sit in a circle, cross-legged and one foot apart from each other.

Place a pencil in the center of the circle. Designate a goal line or object, such as a chair in the far corner of the room.

Say: **We're going to play a fun relay game called Pencil Point. When we're ready to start playing, I'll gently spin the pencil like this.** Demonstrate. **When the pencil stops spinning and is pointed at you, you're "It"!**

You'll run as fast as you can to [the designated object or goal line] **and back without bumping into anyone. If you bump into anyone, you'll have to go back to the circle and wait to be chosen again. When you get back to the circle, spin the pencil quickly to find the next "It." If the pencil points to someone who has already had a turn, spin the pencil a second time. If after three spins, you still haven't chosen a new player, quickly point to someone with your finger. I'll be watching the clock because the object of Pencil Point is for us to beat the clock. We'll start with thirty seconds per player.**

When the last person has returned to the circle, say this chant together:

Three, five, seven, nine—
Don't you think we can beat our time?

Play the game a second time, trying to beat the time you accomplished.

After the second round, say this chant together:
The second round was (or was not) **our best,**
But I'm ready to give this game a rest!

Kids should be ready to rejoin a lesson with their wiggles conquered!

Gospel Rap

All ages

You'll see kids begin to fill their own time with this active partner game.

This game requires two people but can be used for any number of people in pairs or in circle groups.

Two players face each other and recite the following words while hitting hands together with their partners in specific ways (see the key on p. 32 for hand motions).

Matthew,	Matthew,
Matthew,	Mark,
Mark,	Matthew,
Mark.	Luke,
Matthew,	Matthew,
Matthew,	Mark,
Luke,	Luke, and
Luke,	John.

Once your kids get the hang of it with their own partners, have everyone form a double circle with the outer ring facing in and the inner ring facing out. Have the kids pair up with their new partners and work together to get the words and motions correct. Then have the inner circle move one partner to the right and try it again.

For an extra challenge, try speeding up the rap each time you say it. Stop when the class is either out of breath or laughing too hard to continue!

TRY THIS

Challenge the kids to learn other short segments of names of Bible books, substituting them for Matthew, Mark, Luke, and John.

Have kids practice the following hand motions that go with each word of the rap:

Matthew

Mark

Luke

John

Daniel Escapes

Early elementary

Provide kids a welcome opportunity to stretch while re-minding them of a favorite Bible hero.

Begin by clearing the center of your classroom of all furniture and equipment. Make sure that there is plenty of space in the middle of the room and that no one can fall on any hard objects or sharp corners. (You may also take this game outdoors.)

Say: **In the church we all need each other. It's important that we help one another stand strong in our faith. In the Bible, Daniel's obedience to God encouraged other Israelites to stand firm in their faith. We're going to practice helping one another stand strong today with a game.**

Have all of the kids stand in a circle and hold hands. (If you have a large group, you can have kids form more circles.) Choose one student to be the "lion" and go into the center of the circle. Tell the rest of the students that they are Daniel and his friends who are trying to stand firm for God.

Tell kids that when you say "go," the lion should try to break through a pair of hands in the circle. If the lion is successful, the kids on both sides of the break will become lions, too, and will go to the center of the circle.

Play the game, and keep repeating it until there are too few kids left in the circle to connect around all of the lions.

Then have the kids talk about how it felt to rely on the people next to them. Ask:

● **How did you feel when more and more of your friends became lions?**

● **What was it like when your neighbor couldn't hold on?**

● **How is this like or unlike how we depend on each other at church?**

TRY THIS

For a tamer version of this "liony" game, have the lion try to crawl between the legs of two partners instead of breaking their grasp. Have kids in the circle try to keep the lions in with their legs.

TRY THIS

For older kids, this game can be an excellent launch for a discussion on friendship. Use Ecclesiastes 4:9-10, 12 to study the importance of friendships and Christ-like relationships.

Slithering Snake

BEST FOR All ages

Play this indoor variation of the Dog Who Chased His Own Tail to burn excess energy in a hurry.

TRY THIS

Supercharge this game by moving to a grassy area outdoors. Make sure there are no rocks in the play area. Have kids group together with others of similar size (about five kids to a group works well). Have group members stand and hold onto each other by the waist and run after the tail instead of crawling.

Have the kids kneel down on all fours and form a line in a wide open area. Have each child grasp the ankles of the next person in line. When the leader says "go," the head of the snake (the first person in line) races around and tries to catch the tail of the snake (the last person in line). When the head catches the tail—or if the line breaks—everyone should reconnect, and the second person in line becomes the head while the former head moves to the end of the line.

Tunnel Relay

BEST FOR All ages

"Tunnel" under partners in this fun relay race.

Use masking tape to make start and finish lines at opposite ends of the room. Have kids form pairs, and have each pair stand at the start line with the first person's heels against the line, facing the finish line. The first person's legs should be farther apart than shoulder distance. When you say "go," have the second person in each pair crawl under the legs of the first person and then stand up with his or her legs apart so the second person can crawl under. Pairs will continue moving in this manner across the room until all pairs reach the finish line.

PLAYMASTER'S POINTERS

While this game is fun for all ages to play, it works best when the children are of similar size and age. Otherwise it can become a "horsy ride" for the smaller children in the tunnel!

Then have all pairs join together to form a single line with their legs far enough apart for everyone to slither under. Start with the last person in line. As soon as that person gets under the next person's legs, the second person may begin. When the first person gets to the beginning of the line, he or she may stand up and become part of the tunnel. Play is complete when the whole team has crawled through the tunnel and everyone is standing up.

Flash and Freeze

 Early elementary

Transition to a quieter time with this peppy game for younger kids.

Say: **In this game, whenever you see the lights flash off and on, you need to freeze wherever you are. I'll tell you what to do when everyone is frozen. In between "flashes," you can walk around and talk and do whatever you want (within the limits of our class rules).**

Have the kids get up and move around the room. Depending on the number of children and the amount of furniture, you may even encourage them to run around.

At various intervals, flash the lights off and on. When all the kids freeze, give them one of the following directions or make up some fun directions of your own!

- **Scratch a back eight times!**
- **Shake three people's hands!**
- **Hug a friend gently.**
- **Give a nice back rub.**

When it's time to start quieting down, have the kids do the following:

- **Lean against the wall with three people.**
- **Lie on your back alone, and take five deep breaths.**
- **Sit cross-legged in one big circle.**

Play this game with younger children when you study Noah's ark (Genesis 6-8). Each time you stop the kids, yell out the name of an animal they should act out.

With older children, you can teach the story of the ten plagues (Exodus 7-11) by calling out different plagues (frogs—8:1-15; gnats—8:16-19; flies—8:20-32) and, finally, the exodus (have them run for it!) for the kids to act out.

Shoe Biz

Spend some extra energy in this game for busy feet.

Have kids form two teams. Use chalk or tape to make a line down the center of the room, and have one team get on each side of the line.

Have each person take off one shoe and put it in the middle of his or her team's half of the room. Explain to the kids that you will give them two minutes to get all of the shoes out of their team's "territory" and across the line into the other team's territory. Of course the other team will be attempting to do the same thing at the same time.

Say: **The only way you can move a shoe is to slip it on your bare foot and *walk* it over. You must keep your hands clasped behind your back at all times. The shoe does not have to be completely on your foot. You have to set the shoe in the other team's territory without flipping or kicking it. And you must try to block the other team from depositing their shoes on your side. In fact, you can pass their shoes *back* to them. Remember to work together with your teammates. You want as few shoes as possible on your side after two minutes.**

When the game is over, have all of the kids sit in a circle. Start passing shoes hand to hand around the circle. Say: **When your shoe gets to you, keep it; yell, "My shoe!"; and put it on. Stay in the circle, though, so you can keep passing the other shoes until everyone has found his or her own!**

Human Basketball

All ages

Kids take aim in this everyone-takes-a-shot indoor basketball game.

Have kids form teams of no more than eight. Designate one person in each team to be the "basket" and one person to be the "runner." Ask the basket to stand tall with his or her arms forming a basket. The basket may not move at any time. Next have teams line up, scattered diagonally (see illustration).

Give the first person in each line three paper wads to serve as the basketballs. Tell kids that the first person in each line will toss the ball to the next person in the line, and that person will toss it to the next, and so on. If someone drops the ball while tossing it, he or she must walk the ball back to the beginning. When the ball gets to the end, the last person will shoot and try to get a basket. If the basket is made, the team gets two points. The basket person will then run to the other end of the line, and all the players in line will move up one position.

The runner will run the balls back to the beginning of the line. Encourage the kids to try to have all three balls going at once.

Have the kids play. At the end of three minutes, add the points scored by all the teams to see if they broke one hundred. If so, everyone wins! If not, try again.

Heels-to-Toes Race

Children learn to "stick together" in this game of balance and fun.

TRY THIS

When the first pair returns to the start line, a new member may be added to the group, making three people standing heels to toes. The trio may then race to the other side of the room and change positions to race back to the start line. Another person may be added each time until all students are joined heels to toes, racing as one big group.

Rather than having the team return to the start line each time the heels-to-toes connection is broken, you may just want to celebrate the number of steps taken. Encourage the players to develop a strategy for staying together.

Have children form two single-file lines at one end of a hall or classroom. Begin with the first child in each line pairing off together, with one partner standing behind the other, facing front to back. The child facing the partner's back must touch his or her toes to the heels of the partner at all times. To help with balance, the partner standing behind might want to hold the partner's waist or shoulders (see illustration).

On "go," the first pair will carefully race to the other side of the room. If the heels and toes of the pair are not touching at all times, it must begin again at the start line. When the partners reach the finish, they will switch positions and return to the start line. They will touch the next pair and then go to the end of their lines. You can have several teams start at once if you have the space to place them five to ten yards apart.

Speed is not the main focus of this game. Instead, emphasize cooperation and team play.

Up-and-Down Relay

All ages

This game allows kids a quick break from their ordinary routine.

Have the students form a single-file line facing a row of five chairs. Place a piece of paper and a pencil on each chair. When you say "go," the first person in line runs to the first chair, picks up the pencil and paper, sits down, and writes his or her name on the piece of paper. He or she then gets out of the chair, placing the paper and pencil back on the seat, and repeats the same routine on each and every chair.

As soon as the first player in line sits in the second chair, the second player may go. The third person in line must watch for the second person to move to the second chair before he or she may go. The game continues until everyone has added his or her name to each list.

For older students, refocus thoughts on the lesson by having each player write one word about the Bible story or concept you are teaching. For example, if your lesson is about Nehemiah rebuilding the temple wall, the first student in line might write "Nehemiah," the second might write "helped," the third might write "temple," the fourth might write "Ezra," the fifth might write "re-build." The kids cannot repeat a word that already has been written. When all the children have had a turn, read the papers and ask each child to elaborate on what he or she wrote. You can review a previous lesson in this way, too, to check for long-term understanding.

PLAYMASTER'S POINTERS

There's no rule about the number of chairs to set up. Use three chairs if you want to do the activity more quickly or eight if you want to give kids a little more time to burn excess energy.

Line Up

Here's a wiggle-buster for inside days.

How much energy children burn off during this game depends on how fast you pace the questions, making them scramble to get on the line, and whether you ask children to pair-share their responses.

To have kids burn off maximum energy, skip the pair-shares, and include rapid-fire questions like these:

- What do you think of spelling?
- Your family?
- Hamburgers?
- Frozen yogurt?
- Eggplant?
- Bowling?
- Vacations?

Say: **Showing your thoughts, opinions, and feelings isn't always easy. Now that you've learned this game, you can use the same strategy by yourself as you are trying to make decisions or understand yourself better.**

Place a nine-foot piece of masking tape on the floor. At one-foot intervals, place ten-inch pieces of tape diagonally on the long piece of tape, and then number the shorter pieces so that each represents a number from one to ten.

Explain: **I'm going to ask you to go stand on this line soon. *Where* you stand depends on how you answer my question. If your answer is "awful," you'll stand on the 1. If your answer is "wonderful," you'll stand on the 10. If your answer is "average," you'll stand on the 5. You also can stand on the other numbers in between, depending on how strongly you feel. If people are standing where you want to stand, squeeze as close as possible to them without pushing. Ready? Let's practice.**

How was your week? If it was wonderful, stand on the 10. If it was awful, stand on the 1. If it was an absolutely average week, stand on the 5.

When children have found a spot on the line, ask them to turn to a partner and quickly explain why they chose to stand where they did.

Ask children to step off the line and then pick a spot for the following questions:

- **What do you think of school?**
- **What do you think of our class?**
- **How much do you like to play sports?**
- **What do you think of chili dogs?**

Weave Away!

Early or middle elementary

Kids enjoy working together as they complete this high-energy challenge.

Kids can play this game outside or in a large indoor area. Designate a goal line at one end of your area, and have kids line up single file at the opposite end of the area, facing the goal line. Have kids spread out so there is at least one arm's length between each of them.

Have the person at the end of the line farthest from the goal weave his or her way toward the goal, passing between the kids in the line, going to the right of the first, the left of the second, and so on. Once the first person reaches the front of the line, he or she becomes the first person in the line. As soon as this person has taken his or her place, the person now at the farthest end of the line may begin weaving through the line in the same way to reach the front. Keep the line going until all the kids reach the goal. You may want to have the line bend around and head back to where kids started.

Play the game at least two or three times to allow kids to run off energy and improve their performance.

TRY THIS

To add excitement and variation to this game, you could have kids run backward or sideways, crawl on their hands and knees, tiptoe, or slither on their stomachs.

Row, Ride, and Run

BEST FOR Early elementary

Use this fun song to channel kids' wiggles into energetic motions.

Have kids stand and sing the following song while energetically doing motions to fit the first line of each verse.

Row, row, row, your boat
Gently down the stream.
Merrily, merrily, merrily, merrily,
Life is but a dream.

Ride, ride, ride your bike
Smoothly down the street.
Merrily, merrily, merrily, merrily,
Life is such a treat.

Run, run, run your legs
Quickly round the track.
Merrily, merrily, merrily, merrily,
There's no turning back.

March, march, march your feet
Sharply all the way.
Merrily, merrily, merrily, merrily,
It's a happy day.

Hop, hop, hop away,
Bouncing down the trail.
Merrily, merrily, merrily, merrily,
God will never fail.

PLAYMASTER'S POINTERS

You might want to encourage kids to come up with their own verses to the song.

Have kids sing through the song once and do all the actions. Then have kids go through the song one or more times, speeding up or slowing down the words and the actions each time.

Toss and Tag

Upper elementary

Keep this game moving to maximize the challenge for your kids.

Have kids form groups of no more than six. Hand one person from each group a sheet of paper. Have the rest of each group form a circle around the person with the paper.

Say: **Each person in the center needs to form a ball with the sheet of paper. This is a Tag game in which the person in the center is "It." Those of you on the outside must stay in a circle, but you can duck, bob, and weave all you want. "It" must throw the paper ball into the air, touch one of you while the ball is still in the air, and then catch the ball. If "It" can do that, the person who is tagged is the new "It." If not, It will try again.**

For a getting-acquainted version of this game, have "It" begin naming all the people in the group. The last person's name to be said before "It" catches the paper ball is the new "It."

Balance Buddies

All ages

Try this partner game any time and anyplace to challenge your kids' balancing skills.

Have kids form two equal groups. Have one group form a circle, and have the second group form a circle around the first group. Instruct kids in the inner circle to face the kids in the outer circle.

Say: **This is a game of great skill, cooperation, and balance. You'll need to listen carefully to each direction I give. After each direction, you will change partners by moving one person to the right.**

Give the following directions (and others as you think of them):

● **Take one small step backward and touch foreheads**

with your partner.

- Take one foot off the ground and touch pinkie fingers.
- Turn around and touch left shoulder blades.
- Face each other and touch the right soles of your feet together.
- Bend your knees and touch noses.
- Lift one foot up and touch both elbows together.

By this time, your kids should have gotten close to lots of their classmates. Pick up the pace of the instructions as kids improve their skills, or have kids stand farther and farther apart for an extra challenge.

Bippity-Boppin'

BEST FOR Upper elementary

Kids keep hoppin' as they keep a paper ball bippity-boppin'.

Have kids form pairs, and give each pair a piece of paper to form into a ball.

Explain that the object of the game is to keep the paper balls from hitting the ground, using any part of their bodies except their hands. Kids can bump the balls to their partners with their knees, feet, elbows, heads, or forearms, but they can only touch the ball with their hands if it lands on the ground. Have kids keep track of the number of times they pass the ball back and forth without dropping it.

After partners have passed the ball ten times, have them join with another pair that has passed ten times to form a group of four. Let group members devise their own strategy for keeping up the ball. One team may pass it around the circle; another may let whoever is closest pass it to someone else. When a group reaches fifteen passes, have it add more people to the group. Pause every few minutes to allow the kids to re-form groups if they would like to.

Just for fun, try the game with the whole group.

TRY THIS

Let pairs try to move to a specific goal or place while passing the ball back and forth.

Tornado Alley

All ages

Active kids become swirling tornadoes in this game with tight boundaries of fun.

Have kids form two groups of equal numbers. Have each group form a line, facing the other group. Then have each group "expand" so kids in each line are standing with their hands joined and their arms fully extended, forming an alley between the two groups. If your group is large enough, they can make a winding alley instead of a straight one.

PLAYMASTER'S POINTERS

This game is best when played with a large group and really needs at least ten players to be fun.

The first child in each line will pair off together, grasping each other's shoulders. Then these two children will begin turning in a circle, working their way down the alley that has been created by their classmates. When they come to the end of the alley, they will separate and rejoin their lines. Then the second tornado can form at the front of the line.

Kids can either play until everyone has had a turn or until the whole group covers a specified distance.

Rat Trap

Upper elementary

Kids must react quickly to keep from being trapped in this human maze.

Have the kids stand in four equal rows, with about three feet between each row. The children in each row should join hands to form a wall for a maze. Choose one player to be the "caller," one to be the "rat," and one to be the "cat."

When the caller calls out "run," the rat must start running through the rows of the human maze. When the caller calls out "cat," the cat must begin chasing the rat through the maze. When the caller yells out "trap," the players forming the walls of the maze must drop each other's hands and quickly grasp the hands of the people who are in the rows across so the direction of the running space changes.

The caller calls out "trap" at his or her discretion to switch the direction of the maze. If the rat doesn't switch directions immediately, he or she will be trapped by the cat. When the cat catches the rat, the cat becomes the new rat. Choose new players to be the cat and the caller.

Crisscross Applesauce

Upper elementary

Kids crisscross the room to rejoin their teams as quickly as they can.

Have kids form four equal teams, and assign one team to each corner of the room. Then have team members choose an order in which to stand. They may stand in order by date of birth, age, height—any order they can remember is fine.

When you call out "crisscross," the teams must cross to the other side of the room diagonally and regroup in order in opposite corners. When you call out, "Crisscross applesauce," the teams must go to the center of the room, then make a right turn, and then regroup in order in the appropriate corners. If you say, "Applesauce crisscross," teams must go to the center and turn left to find their new corners.

As soon as a group is reassembled in the right spot, they are to call out, "Crisscross applesauce! You can try, but you can't trick us!"

This game gets really interesting when two teams are both certain they're in the right corner but they're in the *same* corner! In this case, have both teams return to their original corners and walk through the change slowly.

Paper-Passin' Pals

Upper elementary

Kids put their feet together to discover the fastest way to deliver papers.

Play this game in a room that has been cleared of obstacles (unless you want to leave a couple of obstacles to create a course for the game). Have each child choose a partner.

Say: **When you deliver newspapers, it's very important to get them to the customers' doors undamaged. Otherwise the customer can call the newspaper office and report that the paper was delivered in poor condition. To help you train for this important assignment—in case you should ever have to deliver newspapers—I have developed a practice course that you can work with a partner. But since this needs to be a little harder than any challenge you might really face, you and your partner are responsible for delivering this paper to the classroom door without using your hands. In fact you may use only your feet. Actually, each of you may use only one foot!**

At the end of the room opposite the door, have each pair sit down on the floor, side by side, with their legs extended. Give each pair a sheet of paper. Have each partner bend the leg that is not touching his or her partner's leg so that the partners can hold the paper between each other's feet (see illustration). Then partners must figure out how to maneuver themselves across the room to drop the paper at the door undamaged.

You'll see all kinds of contortions as each pair attempts to deliver its paper. You may wish to challenge the group to accomplish the paper deliveries using another method, continuing to use one foot from each of the partners. For example, all the pairs could line up across the room, and the kids could pass their papers conveyor-belt style!

TRY THIS

Once all the pairs have delivered their papers, challenge them to join together with another group and figure out how to deliver two papers at once, using every member of the new group!

Gauntlet

BEST FOR All ages

Kids must anticipate the actions of others to get out of the gauntlet.

Have kids form two teams, and have the teams stand in parallel lines, facing each other. Then have all the kids begin this simple clap rhythm in unison: Clap knees, clap knees, clap hands, clap hands. Kids must continue clapping this rhythm throughout the game.

Choose one player to be "It." "It" will move up and down the line, suddenly stop in front of one player, and thrust a hand forward. The player in the gauntlet must thrust a hand forward at the same time. If the players both thrust out the same hand, the player in the gauntlet becomes the new "It." If players thrust out opposite hands, the old "It" continues on to another player.

Egyptian Pull

Upper elementary

There's no rope in this Tug of War game drawn from the traditions of Egypt.

Have kids form groups of six. Lay a strip of masking tape on the floor. Have three people in each group go to one side of the tape and three go to the other side. Each trio should stand in a single-file line facing the tape. The person from each trio who's closest to the tape should grasp hands with the same player from the opposing team. The people behind each of them should grasp the waist of the person in front of them. On "go," each trio should try to bring the opposite trio across the tape line without breaking the grip of the two trio members in front.

Play the game two more times with each member of the trio taking a turn in the front.

A Little Swing

All ages

Kids shake out the wiggles with this fun action chant.

Have the kids stand with partners, scattered around the room. Then teach kids this chant along with the motions:

Hands on your head now. *(Move head from side to side with a hand on each side of the head.)*

Hands on your nose. *(Move head up and down with hands on nose.)*

Hands on your shoulders. *(Circle shoulders with hands on them.)*

Hands on your toes. *(Reach down and touch toes while lifting feet off the floor one at a time.)*

Do a little side step. *(Turn side to side with a partner and step out and in.)*

Do a little swing. *(Rotate entire upper body from the waist.)*

God wants me to praise him *(lift hand over head and sway from side to side)*

In each and every thing. *(Jump up and down.)*

TRY THIS

Have kids make up their own set of motions and teach them to each other.

Do this action chant any time your kids need a movement break.

FRIEND
BUILDERS

Friend Builders bring kids together. They'll get to know
new friends and get better acquainted with old ones as
they play together. Use these games often to help kids establish deep and lasting relationships within God's family.

Table for a Party of ???

Early elementary

Kids will enjoy a fine dining experience with their animal friends in this wacky game.

Turn over a table or designate an outside area as the table. Whisper an animal name to every child in your class. Make sure you assign the same animal to two or more children. Be sure no one tells his or her animal name to anyone else. The object of the game is for the children to find their partner or partners, hold hands, run to the table, and be seated together. The tricky part is that no one knows for sure how many should be in their party.

Explain that at your signal, children should make noises and act like the animals they were assigned. When they find each other, they should be seated at the table. After the first round is completed, reassign animals and play again.

PLAYMASTER'S POINTERS

Here are some suggestions for animal assignments: pig, cow, horse, owl, sheep, dog, cat, rooster, frog, duck, turkey, lion.

My Very Favorite Friend

All ages

Have fun getting to know each other and remembering significant details about friends.

The goal of this game is to use your memory and your physical speed at the same time. You must catch a paper ball in the air before it hits the ground and use your memory about other people as you get rid of the ball again.

Have the kids work together to wad up several sheets of paper into one good-sized ball—about the size of a softball. Then have the kids sit down in a circle and quickly share their answers to one friend-making question. Here are a few to get you started:

- **What's your name?**
- **What school do you go to?**
- **What is your favorite subject in school?**
- **What's your favorite ice cream flavor?**

PLAYMASTER'S POINTERS

After the kids have had a chance to share their answers, gather the whole group. Say: **Now you'll get a chance to test your memory using the information your friends just shared with you. We'll start the game answering the question "What's your name?"**

If your kids are already somewhat acquainted with one another, you can have them share answers to two or three questions at a time to make the game more challenging. If you have lots of brand-new kids, start with the most basic questions such as "What's your name?" and only do one question at a time.

Have one player hold on to the paper ball and stand in the middle of the playing area. This player will call out another child's answer to the question and throw the ball as high as he or she can. For example, if the question is "What's your name?" the player may call out "Sally," knowing that one of the other children is named Sally.

Then Sally will rush in and catch the ball before it lands on the ground. If the ball hits the ground before Sally catches it, she must return to the circle. If Sally catches the ball, she'll throw the ball into the air as she calls out another child's answer to the question.

If a name or other answer is called out to which more than one child can respond, all of them can go for the ball. For example, if MacArthur Elementary is called out in the "What school do you go to?" category, the one person from MacArthur who catches the ball becomes "It." *But* if he or she drops the ball, all of the kids who attend MacArthur must sit back down, and the same player remains "It."

After you have played two or three rounds of this game, you can make the game more challenging by using the answers from two or more rounds at the same time. In this variation, the person in the middle could call out a name, a school, or a favorite food at any time!

Matthew, Mark, Luke, and John

 **BEST FOR** Upper elementary

This game is especially good for kids with logical or mathematical learning styles.

TRY THIS

Use this same game to learn each other's names. Have the members of each group share their names again and decide whose name will replace each number. Having to concentrate on the other players' names and repeat them again and again is not only fun, but it also helps the kids plant their new friends' names in their brains forever! As a visual clue for this variation, have each child hold up the number of fingers his or her name is replacing.

PLAYMASTER'S POINTERS

Talk with the kids about why it's important to learn each other's names. We should care enough about each other to get to know one another. After all, the God of the universe knows each of us personally. He even knows the number of hairs on our heads (Matthew 10:30).

Have kids sit in circles of four to six, and have kids share their names with each other.

Next ask the kids to take turns counting as they go around the circle. However, to make it a little bit more exciting (and difficult) have them use the names of the authors of the Gospels in place of certain numbers. Every time a 1 comes up, replace it with "Matthew." For example, the number 11 would be Matthew-Matthew. Instead of 2, use "Mark." Replace the number 3 with "Luke." And use "John" instead of the number 4. (So 34 would be Luke-John.) Post this code on the board or on newsprint so the kids have a reference point:

Matthew = 1
Mark = 2
Luke = 3
John = 4

Have the group try to count to 100 without making any mistakes. Every time someone goofs, though, the group must start over at the beginning. The counting would go as follows: Matthew, Mark, Luke, John, 5, 6, 7, 8, 9, Matthew-0, Matthew-Matthew, Matthew-Mark, and so on all the way to 100 (or rather, Matthew-0-0).

Jamaquack Jamboree

All ages

Your kids will "quack up" with this fun and creative game.

From the faraway land of Oceanalia comes this game based on one of their rare native birds. Have your class form a large circle, or "pen," and hold hands. Appoint six members of your class to be the first group of Jamaquacks. They should move into the center of the circle while the rest of the class rejoins hands in the circle. The Jamaquacks should bend over and grab their ankles or calves. Then the Jamaquacks should shuffle around backward inside the pen. Whenever a Jamaquack bumps into another Jamaquack, they should reach through their legs, shake hands, and introduce themselves. After the first group of Jamaquacks has had a chance to meet each other, let another group of six children take their place.

Kids could play this game for a long time as the groups of six re-form with new members (with some who may have been Jamaquacks together already).

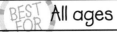

TRY THIS

Kids can play this game all together as long as you have a well-defined space where kids won't run into anything but each other.

Meet in the Middle

All ages

Help kids discover how much they have in common with this "ice-breaking" game.

Have your class form a circle around the room. When you call out a phrase that describes them, tell them to walk into the middle of the circle and introduce themselves to everyone else in the middle. Start by naming items of clothing such as blue jeans or plaid shirts, and then move to hobbies or favorite foods the kids might have. You can also use phrases such as "one sibling" or "home schooled," "math whiz," or "book lover."

After the kids have had a chance to meet in the middle, go back to your list of categories, and have kids give a high five to someone in each category you call out. Each high-five group can have any number of members but must have at least one person who went to the middle for that category during the first part of the game. For example, if you call out the category "one sibling," everyone who has only one sibling should raise both hands, and the rest of the group will run to these individuals to give them a high five and become part of that child's high-five group. This individual signifies that he or she is the "middleman" by holding up both hands. When everyone is in a high-five group, have all the kids return to the circle; then re-call another category. This stage of the game increases the chances that all children will interact at some point during the game.

Shake It Up!

BEST FOR **All ages**

Unique handshakes help kids identify their similarities and differences.

TRY THIS

Once your kids are familiar with this activity, you can also use it to mix age levels for multi-age activities. Have the kids shake hands the number of times that corresponds with their grade but not link with *anyone* that shakes hands the same number of times. You can tell kids to find one person from *each* of the six grades if your group is larger or just three or four kids from different grades if your group is smaller.

Have kids number off, starting with one and using as many numbers as necessary to ensure that there are about three to five kids for each number. Then explain that everyone in the group will walk around and greet one another without talking.

Tell the "ones" to greet others by shaking hands one time, the "twos" to shake hands two times, and so on. The fun part of this activity comes when a one or two wants to stop shaking hands while his or her partner, who is a three, wants to continue. Remind the kids that there's no talking!

When kids with the same numbers find each other, have them link up and work together to seek out the remaining kids with the same number.

When all the kids in one group are found, have them sit down and learn about each other. In a younger age group, ask kids to share their favorite foods, their pets' names, and the number of brothers or sisters. Have older kids share a favorite song or musician, their hobbies, and a favorite sport. Make sure everyone knows each other's name by the end of the round!

What's My Name?

BEST FOR **All ages**

Mix reviewing the Bible and getting to know each other in this name game.

Start out by having kids brainstorm for various favorite Bible characters. Have kids share whether their character is from the Old or New Testament, was male or female, a good guy or a bad guy, and some basic events of his or her life. Make sure that lots of different characters are discussed. For younger children, write these characters' names on the board, and leave them for all to see during the game.

Let each child pick a favorite character (for younger children, limit them to only using the ones just discussed), and write the character's name on a piece of blank paper. Have the child choose someone else in the room and tape the name on that person's back without letting the other child see the name.

Also instruct each child to write his or her own name on another piece of paper and use masking tape to attach it to his or her own *front*.

Say: **The object of this game is to ask questions to find out what Bible name you've been given. You may ask only questions that can be answered with a simple "yes" or "no." For example, "Am I a good guy?"— not "Am I a good guy or a bad guy?"**

You may ask as many questions as you want, but ask each person only one question at a time. After you ask someone a question, you may go back to

TRY THIS

Have kids create signs that are biblical pairs such as David and Goliath, Cain and Abel, Adam and Eve, and Jacob and Esau. In this variation, kids need to discover who they are *and* find their "partner" in the crowd.

You could also use this activity as a class party or review game at the end of a series of lessons. You can write out the Bible names ahead of time. Use the key characters from the last several lessons your class has studied together. Asking and answering questions about the characters will help refocus the kids' brains on the content of your recent lessons.

someone you have already asked.

You must use the real name of the person you're speaking to every time you ask a question. For example, ask, "Sally, am I from the New Testament?" You must *never* answer a question if the person forgets to use your name as part of the question.

You must answer all questions truthfully, but it's OK to say, "I don't know" if you can't answer a question. As soon as you think you know whose name is on your back, you may ask someone and get a "yes" or "no" answer.

The Lost Sheep

BEST FOR **Upper elementary**

Try this game in a group that "baa-rely" knows each other.

To prepare ahead of time, cut or tear paper into pieces. Write on each piece "sheep" or "lost sheep." Only have a few lost sheep, about one for every four group members. Have each child draw a piece, and ask kids to keep what's written on their pieces to themselves. Say: **As you came in, you each received a piece of paper with something written on it. Some of you are sheep, and a few of you are lost sheep. It is the job of each of you to find the lost sheep. Take a few minutes to introduce yourselves to each other and ask who is lost. As you search, make sure you remember the names of the people who are lost.**

Tell kids how many lost sheep there are, and let them play. After about two minutes, ask the group who the lost sheep are, and see how many kids found the lost sheep. Say: **Just as we looked for the lost sheep in our group, Jesus is looking for "lost sheep": the people he knows who don't know him. Jesus knows their names already, and he loves each one of them. And just as we looked for the lost sheep in this game, we should also help find lost sheep in our world and introduce them to Jesus. It's great to learn the names of people who are here in our little sheep pen, but we need to find those who are outside and need to know the love of God, too.**

Is That Me?

Early or middle elementary

Help children learn more about each other and feel good about themselves.

Say: **The Bible tells us that when someone becomes a Christian, he or she becomes a new person. This new person acts and thinks more and more like Jesus.** Let's think of some ways a person might act and think like Jesus. Brainstorm with the children, and list on a chalkboard or newsprint some positive quality descriptions such as "generous," "loves others," "helpful," "happy," "patient," "loves God," or "friendly."

Have each child write his or her name on a half sheet of paper, fold it once, and put it in a container. Then have each child draw a name from the container, keeping the name secret. Give each child another piece of paper.

Say: **On your piece of paper, write a sentence or two about the person whose name is on your card. Think of ways that person acts or thinks like Jesus. Write your name at the bottom, and put the paper back in the container.** Help those who need assistance.

Choose a description from the container, and read it aloud without naming the person. Then ask the group to try to identify the person described. The child who wrote the description can't give it away!

Give one point for each correct identification. If a child recognizes his or her own description, give the whole group double points.

Color Me Friend

All ages

Help your visual learners remember details about new or old friends.

Give each person a crayon, and then tell the kids to look at the name of their crayon's color. Next have the kids arrange themselves in alphabetical order according to the name of the crayon color (or from light to dark colors for children who are not yet reading). When the line is complete, have the kids turn to the person on either side and tell something about themselves that reminds them of their color. For example, kids could say, "Red—like red roses" or "Blue—my favorite fruit is blueberries."

Have the kids trade crayons and repeat the activity several times. Then collect the crayons. Show each crayon one by one, and have the kids share something they remember about another person in the group that was related to that color.

It's All in Your Name

All ages

Linguistic learners will enjoy affirming others in this game that emphasizes their particular gift.

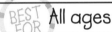

TRY THIS

Kids might enjoy transferring their names and descriptions to a separate piece of paper to keep as an encouragement.

On the chalkboard, dry-erase board, or a large sheet of newsprint, write the names of each child vertically. Have kids form groups of three and ask each other questions to help them fill in the letters of the person's name using words that describe him or her. Kids can ask questions about each other's favorite animal, color, sport, game, number, food, or any other favorite they might think of. Kids also may use words that describe personality traits such as "nice," "understanding," "friendly," and so on. Each group of three will try to be the first to fill in all three of their names.

This is a fun and affirming way to learn each others' names and what makes each of us unique!

Favorite Things

All ages

Kids combine dramatic flair with getting-to-know-you facts in this fun acting game.

Hand out a small strip of paper and a pencil to each student. Instruct kids to write a few words about something very special in their lives You might suggest a favorite pet, a special birthday party, or a vacation to the beach. Let the children find their own private spots in the room so that no one else sees what they're writing. Allow kids one minute to come up with their "favorite thing."

When time is up, have kids fold their papers, and have half of the students deposit their papers into your cupped hands. The other half of the students should hold on to their papers and also draw another paper from your hands. These children should open their papers and try to find the person who wrote it. Once a student has located the author, the two should sit down together.

Then have the pairs think of a way to silently act out both of their favorites together. For example, if one partner wrote, "My cat" and the other wrote, "Fishing at the lake," they could develop a short scene depicting a cat fishing at the lake or someone fishing with a cat rubbing up against his or her leg. While no words are allowed, kids *can* generate their own sound effects.

Give each pair a chance to perform while the audience tries to guess not only the two favorite things, but also which favorite thing came from which classmate. By the end of the game, kids should know about something special to everyone in the class.

Mix to Match

Help kids expand their friendship base with this game that is perfect for a new school year.

Have kids form groups of four or five, and let each group elect a spokesperson. Allow the group members a minute or two to discover something they all have in common. After time is up, have the small groups gather together to form a circle. Each small group should remain clustered together within the larger circle.

Have one group's spokesperson stand up, introduce himself or herself and the group members, and share their commonality. Then ask the larger group if other students share the same interest. Any student who shares the interest of the presenting group—except the spokesperson for each group—should stand up and run to that group before the rest of the class counts to five. Then the people who have switched groups should introduce themselves. You may have several spokespersons who are left standing alone, but they won't be for long! As each spokesperson reports, the kids will have an opportunity to join a new group.

Ask:

● **What are some things you have to do to make new friends?**

● **What does this game show you about connecting with new people?**

● **How can we help each other make new friends?**

Say: **We always can share our friends by helping to introduce them to others. Sometimes common interests are a great place to start new relationships.**

Opportunity Sculptures

BEST FOR Upper elementary

Kids will use their imaginations to create sculptures from each other.

Have the children gather in a large, cleared area such as the center of the classroom or church hall. Have kids form groups of four to six. Explain the goal of this game is for each group to create a sculpture using only items in their possession at this very moment. This could include chairs kids are sitting in, shoes, sweaters, and their own bodies. Explain that groups will have two minutes to plan and then each group must complete its sculpture without talking. Suggest that instead of speaking, the students rely on demonstrating what they would like another member of the group to do (such as lying in a certain position), using hand signals, or gently urging someone physically into position by leading them by the hand. If personal items, such as shoes and sweaters, are being used to create the image, only the owner of the item is allowed to move that particular object. Set a time limit of five to ten minutes.

After time is up, let other children guess what the sculpture is; then have each group explain the various components of their artistic design.

TRY THIS

Read aloud 1 Corinthians 12:12. Ask kids how their group sculptures were like what is described in this Bible verse. Have the kids discuss in their groups how each person was a part of the total sculpture and how they are part of the total Body of Christ as described in this verse.

Go to Your Corner

This is a great game to use when you have new children in your group or you want your children to get to know each other better.

Gather your kids in the center of the room. Say: **I'm going to ask you to make some choices and then go to a corner depending on what you choose. Let's practice: If you** had your choice of pizza or a salad for lunch, which would you choose? **Pizza over there** (indicate a corner) **and a salad over there** (indicate another corner). **While you're there, tell one person why you chose as you did, and tell the person your name.**

Then gather children back in the center of the room again. Send them to corners with the following questions, and ask them to follow the accompanying directions while in the corners:

● **Would you rather have vanilla ice cream or chocolate ice cream? Tell someone your name and favorite color.**

● **Is your birthday in an even or odd month? Tell someone your name and when you were born.**

● **Would you rather wear shoes with shoelaces or shoes without shoelaces? Tell someone your name and the name of a stuffed animal you once had.**

● **Would you rather take a vacation at the ocean or in the mountains? Tell someone your name and your favorite kind of cookie.**

● **Are you a "cat" person or a "dog" person? Tell someone your name and how many people are in your family.**

● **Would you rather get up early or late? Tell someone your name and your favorite circus act.**

● **Do you squeeze the toothpaste tube from the middle or the end? Tell someone your name and your favorite holiday— and why.**

The Shoe Pile

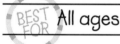

Kids will "shoe"ly learn more about each other as they play this simple game.

Have the children walk around the room, talking to each other and finding out as much about others as they can. If you notice some kids struggling to connect with others, suggest that they ask about favorites—vacation spots, colors, foods, or school subjects, for example. After about five minutes, call everyone together, and ask each student to put one shoe into a pile. Then have everyone sit on the floor in a circle and try to hide their other shoe. Have one person at a time go to the shoe pile, select a shoe that belongs to someone else, try to match it to its owner, and then tell what he or she learned about that person. You can also ask other kids to contribute facts they learned about that person.

Handshake Knot

Kids use each other's names to accomplish their goal in this familiar challenge.

Have everyone stand in a circle with their hands at their sides. When you say "shake," have the kids start shaking the hands of two people at the same time, introducing themselves to those around them. When kids have shaken those hands, they should reach out to people farther away, always shaking hands with two people at the same time. When you say "stop," have everyone keep holding the hands they are shaking at that moment to create the "handshake knot."

To untie the handshake knot, have everyone work together to undo the knot without letting go of hands. Have kids use the names they just learned to direct each other over, under, around, and through arms, hands, and bodies. Tell kids that any request not accompanied by a name should not be carried out.

Circle, Stop, and Tell

BEST FOR Middle or upper elementary

This game gives kids some action as they get better acquainted.

Have kids form two equal groups. Then have one group form a circle facing out and the other group form a second circle, facing in, around the first circle.

Say: **When I say "go," start marching to your left. When I yell, "Stop and tell," you must stop and tell the person across from you one thing about yourself that the person doesn't already know. If you don't end up with someone across from you, you'll need to scramble to find a partner in the other circle who also doesn't have someone across from them. After a few seconds of sharing, I'll again say "go." Then you'll circle in the opposite direction until I shout, "Stop and tell" again.**

TRY THIS

Instead of just saying "go," play some upbeat praise music for the children to march to.

Say "go" to start the game, and let kids march for several seconds before stopping them. Keep the game going until kids have talked to most other kids at least one time. After the game, give kids an opportunity to share with the group interesting things they learned about others.

What Do You Know?

All ages

This game could be the most important three minutes of your class time.

Have kids form pairs with someone they don't know very well. Say: **I'm going to give you about three minutes to learn as much as you can about your partner. At the end of three minutes, we're going to play a game to see how much you've learned.**

After three minutes, have the pairs form a circle around you. Go around the circle, asking one partner in each pair the first question from the list below. If the partner doesn't know the answer to the question, he or she can make up an answer. After each partner answers, have the rest of the kids vote on whether the answer was correct or not. Then have the second partner tell what the correct answer is. After one person from each pair has answered the first question, ask the next question about the opposite partner in each pair. Don't keep score; just have fun with the game as you go along. Keep playing until you run out of questions or until kids begin to lose interest.

● **What color is your partner's favorite food?**
● **Who is your partner's biggest hero?**
● **How many pencils does your partner have?**
● **What is the longest distance your partner has ever ridden a bike?**
● **What is your partner's favorite comic strip?**
● **Can one of your partner's siblings do a handstand?**
● **What is your partner's least favorite school subject?**
● **What would your partner like to do when he or she grows up?**

Say: **Now turn to your partner, and tell him ,or her the thing you learned that was most interesting to you!**

Shoe Detective

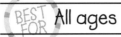

Oh, the tales a shoe could tell if shoes could only talk!

Have kids sit in a circle, take off one shoe, and place it in the middle of the circle.

Say: **When it's your turn, pick a shoe from the pile whose owner you know just a little bit or not at all. Of course, don't take your own shoe!**

Next, while looking very closely at the shoe as a good shoe detective would, make a guess about the shoe's owner. You might say something like "This shoe's owner must be a cool dresser" or "This shoe's owner must like to play outdoors." Whatever you say has to be based on what you think the shoe might say about the owner, and shoes are faithful servants that would never say anything bad about the foot that fills them. Remember, when I point to you, pick a shoe belonging to someone you don't know very well. Then, while holding the shoe, tell us one positive thing that may be true of the owner.

After the detective has made his or her guess, the shoe owner will claim the shoe and tell the group if the shoe clue was true. Then the shoe owner will take the next turn. We will continue until all the shoes have been returned to their owners.

More About You

This twist on Mother May I? helps kids find out more about their classmates.

To start, have kids stand shoulder to shoulder in one line facing you. Stand approximately one hundred feet away from the line of kids.

Say: **We're going to have fun getting to know each other**

better. In this game, you get to move the way I tell you to move only if I've said something true about you. If you are the first one to touch me, you may then take my place as leader. Let's start. You'll catch on quickly.

- If you've ever played on a soccer team, take four "frog leaps" now. (Demonstrate this action if you need to.)
- If you prefer reading a book to watching TV, take five giant steps.
- If you have a younger brother or sister, take six twirls.

Continue until a child touches you. That child takes your place, and the others return to form a new starting line. Help each child who leads come up with different movements such as hopping on one foot, crawling like a baby, or race walking. Every time a player touches the leader, let that person become the new leader. Start over as time allows.

Name Game

 All ages

Actions spark name recall in this get-acquainted game.

Have the kids stand in a circle so that each person can see every other person in the group. Teach the kids this chant:

[Name] **is my name.**
Action is my game.
And if you can't remember it,
Well, that would be a shame!

Choose a person to begin. Have the person say the rhyme, beginning with his or her name, and choose an action to do while saying the rhyme. Some possible actions are bending knees slightly and then standing straight, moving the forearm up and down in front of the face, hopping on one foot, snapping fingers on both hands, and clapping knees. Then the whole group should do the action and repeat the chant back to the person:

[Name] **is her** [or his] **name.**

Action is her [or his] **game.**
And if we can't remember it,
Well, that would be a shame!

Go around the circle, giving each child a turn. Periodically, run behind a person who had an earlier turn, and have the whole group repeat the rhyme and action that person did. When everyone has had a turn, point to each child in random order, and have the rest of the children shout out that child's name as they do the action.

Finger Tag

BEST FOR **All ages**

This contained game of Tag is perfect fun for a small area.

Choose one child to be "It." You may want to write down the following chant so kids can read it until they know it by heart. "It" should stand with his or her hand extended at shoulder height with the palm down. The rest of the children should form a semicircle around "It" and touch his or her palm with only one finger.

"It" will say the following rhyme:

I have a friend, and my friend has me.
I'll meet my friend under yonder tree.
There we'll laugh and have such fun,
And we won't go home til the setting sun.

On the word "sun," "It" will try to grab a finger from those who are touching his or her palm, and the rest of the children will try to jerk back their hands before "It" can touch their fingers. The person whose finger "It" grabs becomes the new "It.

OUTDOOR ADVENTURES

Outdoor Adventures offer your class the opportunity to get out into the fresh air and do what kids do best—*play!* You'll find games to play in the water, snow, and grass.

Kids will run, jump, and search God's creation as they enjoy the great outdoors, whether they're playing at summer camp or in the church parking lot!

Human-Ball Soccer

Middle and upper elementary

This is a low-skill, fun-for-all version of classic soccer.

Set up a small soccer field that's about half the normal size by using kids to mark the goals and the corners of the field. Choose one child to start as the "ball," and have the kids who remain form two teams. A team can include as few as three people.

Say: **This game of soccer will be a little different from any you've ever seen. Since we don't want to hurt our ball, no one will actually be kicking it. To move the ball down the field, the player closest to the ball will shout a command, and the ball will move accordingly. For example, someone might command the ball to move six giant steps to the right or to turn around and move four giant steps forward. The greatest distance a ball can travel in one "kick" is ten giant steps. The "kicker" may not touch the ball or turn it in any way other than through using a single instruction. Also, a kicker may not move the ball more than once in a turn.**

Have kids scatter out on the field, with players from both teams on each side of the field; then place the ball in the middle of the field. Kids are to remain in the same places until a goal is scored. Instruct the ball to keep his or her eyes closed tightly throughout the game.

Choose one of the kids closest to the ball to be the first kicker. You will need to judge which child the ball ends up closest to, and that child will be the next kicker.

When a team scores a goal, reorganize the teams, letting the kids who were markers become players and vice versa. Also be sure to choose a new ball for each game.

PLAYMASTER'S POINTERS

Kids could also play this game indoors in a gymnasium or another large room.

If you don't have enough kids to mark the goals and corners, use any available items to mark the field, and let all the kids participate at once.

Olympic Pool Points

All ages

Kids love to have adults watch them perform pool stunts. Use this guide to create one of the easiest activities you'll ever find to entertain kids.

For your next pool gathering, instead of making up a lot of hard-to-lead games that require various pieces of equipment, just bring paper and magic markers or premade signs with "Olympic" scores—such as "8.6," "9.3," and "9.9"—written on them.

If the pool is in a backyard, use just one or two leaders stationed near part of the pool. If you're using a large community pool, have several pairs of leaders go to various parts of the pool. All the leaders need to do is sit and watch kids dive, jump, do belly-flops, swim laps, dive for toys, hold their breath, do somersaults, do underwater handstands, sit on the bottom of the pool, do synchronized-swimming routines, or perform "freestyle" moves (in other words, whatever stunts kids want to show off!).

Announce the "category" for the next round of competition—for example, biggest splash, quietest dive, or silliest look—and then have leaders hold up signs to score the kids as in Olympic diving competitions, using mostly 9.9s.

Kids will eat up the attention, and adults will love being able to sit. Plus parents will appreciate that you have stationed leaders in various parts of the pool to keep an eye on the kids at all times.

Pool Pass

All ages

Use this game to help eliminate waiting for turns at poolside.

You may also play this game using whatever is handy at your pool party that won't get ruined by the water. Kids' favorites might include a shoe, a towel, an unopened can of soda, or anything else you wouldn't normally let kids take into the pool!

The first person in line takes the object and passes it between his or her legs to the next person in line. That person takes the item and passes it over his or her head to the following person. The third pass goes back between the legs, and so on.

Another great idea would be to use a block of ice and keep passing it until it melts!

Pool parties are naturals for kids, but most pool games require all the kids to stand in the cold while one or two kids at a time are in the pool engaged in the actual game. Here's one game that involves everyone at one time and keeps the whole gang warm!

Tell kids that you're going to have a relay race in the water. Have them line up in single file across the shallow end with their legs spread as far apart as possible. Say: **When I say "go," the first person in line will turn around and swim underwater through the legs of as many people as he or she can. When that person can't swim any farther, he or she will come up for air and get in the line at that place. Then the person at the front of the line will start. Once you reach the other side of the pool, hop out and root for your team to finish.**

Continue the relay until all the players have successfully reached the opposite side of the pool. Each person will finish even if he or she can only swim under one teammate at a time.

Fruit-of-the-Spirit Tag

All ages

Use this game of Tag to help kids remember the fruit of the Spirit found in Galatians 5:22-23.

Choose one person to be "It," and have the rest of the players scatter around the play area. Be sure to establish boundaries so kids don't stray too far away. To play the game, a child who gets tagged by "It" is frozen until touched by another player, who must first call out the name of a fruit of the Spirit. Each fruit of the Spirit may be used only once, so encourage children to loudly call out the fruits.

Continue the game until all the players are frozen. The last person tagged becomes the next "It."

What Time Is It, King Ahab?

Early elementary

Play this game with the story found in 1 Kings 18:44-46 about Elijah running ahead of King Ahab's chariot.

Have kids stand side by side in a line. Choose one child to play the part of King Ahab and stand about thirty feet away from the line with his or her back to the rest of the class. To play the game, the children in the line call out, "What time is it, King Ahab?" Then the king turns around to face the children and calls out a time. If the king calls out, "Ten o'clock," the children take ten steps toward the king; if the king calls out, "Three o'clock," the children take three steps; and so on. Then the king turns his or her back on the children again so they can ask, "What time is it, King Ahab?" Once again, the king turns toward the children and calls out a time.

When the children are close enough, the king responds to their question by saying, "Time for a chariot race." At this point, the king chases the other children back toward the start line. Whoever King Ahab catches first trades places with the king, and the game starts over again with the rest of the children returning to the start line.

The Big Fish

BEST FOR Early elementary

Listening carefully and following directions are the keys to success in this fast-paced game.

Draw or tape three squares on the ground to represent Joppa, Tarshish, and Nineveh. The squares each should be large enough for all of your kids to stand in without much extra room. Make the squares far enough apart so that kids will have to run between the "cities." Identify each city by marking "J," "T," or "N" in the appropriate square.

Select one player to be the "big fish." Say: **All the rest of you are now "Jonahs," and you're in danger of being swallowed by the big fish! You must run fast to avoid being grabbed and gobbled up.**

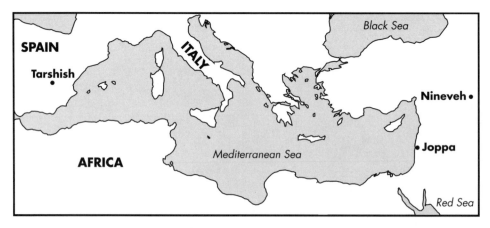

When I yell "Joppa," you must run to the square marked "J" to be safe. When I yell "Tarshish," you must run to the square marked "T," and so on. Pay attention, because you are not safe from the big fish unless you go to the right city. If I call, "Man overboard," you may run to any city you want.

Remember, every time I call for you to go to a new city, you must avoid getting tagged by the big fish. If you do get tagged, you'll become a big fish and help tag other Jonahs.

To make the game more interesting and more realistic, place Joppa and Nineveh fairly close together and Tarshish farther away. Talk with the kids about how Jonah would have been safe traveling the short distance to Nineveh as God had commanded, but instead he chose to flee to Tarshish, which was clear across the Mediterranean Sea. (See Jonah 1–3.)

Spies and Giants

BEST FOR **Any age**

Use this game with the story of the spies and the giants found in Numbers 13.

Mark two lines on the pavement or grass with masking tape. The lines should be twenty to thirty yards apart depending on the ages of your kids. Call one line the "wilderness" and the other line the "Promised Land."

Have kids form two even teams of Israelite spies and Canaanite giants. Have the giants stand on the Promised Land line with their backs to the spies, who should stand on the wilderness line.

When you shout "go," the spies should sneak quickly and quietly toward the giants. When you think they're close enough, yell: **Look out! The giants are coming!**

When you yell, it's the cue for the giants to turn around and chase the spies back to their line. If a spy gets tagged, he or she becomes a giant.

For another round, have the giants sneak up on the spies and the spies turn around to chase the giants back to the Promised Land. It's not necessary to declare a winner or a loser, but if you want to do so, the team with the most players at the end wins.

Hidden Treasures

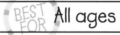 **BEST FOR** Early elementary

This game really appeals to children who excel in naturalistic intelligence.

Say: **In Matthew 13:44, Jesus tells a story about a man who had a great treasure. He loved it so much that he buried it in a field and then bought the field it was in. What would be a treasure that you would love that much?** Allow time for answers. **I think there are many great treasures in this world given to us by God. When God created the world, he said it was good.**

Let's play a game. In this world [or playground, yard, and so on] **are many treasures created by God—for example, leaves and rocks and other stuff you find outside. In the next few minutes, see how many treasures you can find. Then bring them back to the group so we can talk about what you found.**

Let the children search and find their treasures for approximately five minutes. Then bring kids back together to discuss why they believe that the things they found are treasures.

Front to Front

BEST FOR All ages

Kids really get together in this game of following directions.

You'll need an odd number of players for this game. If an even number of kids is present, you'll need to play. Ask for a volunteer to be "It," and have the rest of the kids form pairs and scatter with their partners within a specified area. Then have the partners stand back to back.

To play the game, "It" gives commands such as "front to front," "elbow to elbow," "head to head," each time naming a different body part. Partners change their positions but keep the same partner.

At some point in the game, "It" says, "All change." Then everyone needs to find a new partner. "It" quickly tries to find a partner, leaving someone else to be the new "It."

Call out two different body parts along with a position word—"hand on shoulder," "knee under chin," "foot over hand," or "leg around ankle," for example. This option works best when you give the directions and when kids find new partners with each direction.

Cross the Line

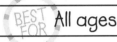 **All ages**

Kids will enjoy this gentler version of Red Rover.

Have kids form two teams, and have each team line up, hold hands, and face the other team. (The teams need to line up about twenty yards apart from each other.) Use masking tape to mark a line down the center of the playing area.

For each round of the game, one team huddles and picks someone to be the "catcher" and picks a person on the other team to call for. When the team has made its choices, they line back up. Then the team begins to chant the following rhyme to the rhythm of the Red Rover chant.

It's time, it's time
To send [child's name] **'cross the line.**

The person whose name is called tries to run across the line and hook up to the other team's chain without being tagged by the catcher. If the person is tagged, he or she must go back to the other side. If the person is able to hook on to the other team's chain, he or she may take someone from the chain back to the other team. Then it's the other team's turn. Play as long as kids are interested.

Plane Race

All ages

Turn paper airplanes into a challenging game.

Before going outside, give each person a piece of plain paper to make an airplane. Most kids can make their own airplanes, but be available to help as well as to encourage the kids to help each other. Each person will need to write his or her name on a paper airplane.

Outside, use masking tape to mark a "takeoff runway" and a "touchdown runway" about twenty yards apart from each other. Have each person start at the takeoff runway and throw his or her plane toward the touchdown runway. Tell the kids to wait until their planes land before picking them up. Then allow kids to pick up their planes, stand where they landed, and throw them again and until they cross the touchdown runway. When everyone has crossed the touchdown runway, the "pilots" have completed their mission.

If some kids have difficulty, match kids in pairs with those who have already finished.

PLAYMASTER'S POINTERS

You may want to give kids a second piece of paper to re-design a plane for a second round.

The Shepherd Loves His Sheep

All ages

Play this game with the parable of the lost sheep found in Matthew 18:10-14.

Have the kids choose who will be the "shepherd," the "shepherd's helper," and the "wolf." The rest of the kids are "sheep." Reserve a corner portion of the play area to serve as the sheep's pen. Reserve the opposite corner to serve as the wolf's den. Have all the sheep count to ten as they spread out. On ten, the shepherd begins the strenuous task of capturing all of his or her wayward sheep, who run away to avoid being tagged.

Once a sheep is tagged, the shepherd's helper brings the sheep to the sheep's pen and guards it from the wolf. If the wolf ventures too close, the shepherd's helper chases and tags the wolf, who then must retreat to his or her den and count to 100 before beginning the chase again.

Since the shepherd, like our Father in heaven, doesn't want any of his sheep to be lost, he or she continues to look for sheep until all are found and are safely in their pen. The game is over when all the sheep are safely in the sheep's pen.

Zip, Zoom, Zowie

BEST FOR Early elementary

Kids will love this freestyle cooperative relay.

Gather the children around you. Say: **We're going to have a relay race—but we'll all be on the same team! We'll start here and run to** [indicate a marker about ten yards away—around a tree or to a piece of paper you've placed on the ground, for example] **and back.**

Please form a single-file line behind me. I'll place a piece of tape on the back of our first runner. When the first runner completes the course, the second runner will take the tape off his or her back, give the tape back to the first runner, and the first runner will place the tape on the second runner's back.

Tell children that they can select their *own* way to do the relay but that each contestant must move in a way that hasn't been used before. Some options include hopping on one foot, hopping on two feet, running, walking backward, skipping, or walking heel to toe. Kids may also consider crawling, slithering, running on their hands and feet like an animal, or even somersaulting.

Add a sense of urgency to the event by timing the game, but be sure the race is against your watch—*not* between children.

Hold a second relay to see if children can improve their time. During the second round, tell children they can do the relay in any way they want, as fast as they can, whether someone has already chosen that movement or not. You'll see a remarkable improvement!

Gather your children around and ask:

● **Which race went fastest? Why did it go faster?**

Read aloud Hebrews 12:1, and then ask:

● **What gets in the way of your following Jesus?**

● **How can you throw off that problem?**

Say: **God wants us to serve him without anything holding us back.**

Recall Tag

BEST FOR **All ages**

Kids will actually enjoy testing their recall with this fun game.

Designate safety zones, about forty feet apart, on each side of a playing field. Have kids form two teams and line up side by side, about ten feet apart, and facing each other in the center of the playing area. Name one team "true" and the other team "false." Ask true-or-false questions about the lesson of the day, and after a pause, say "go!" If the answer to the question is "true," the true team chases the false team, trying to tag a member of that team before that team can reach the safety zone. If the answer to the question is "false," the roles reverse.

Tagged team members become members of the opposite team. If a child leaves before you call "go" or runs the wrong way, he or she becomes a member of the opposite team. Continue the game until one team has been completely absorbed by the opposite team or until time has run out.

Trees, Rocks, and Grass

 Upper elementary

Kids will enjoy playing this active version of the old party game Murder.

Give each child a 1x1-inch piece of paper. All pieces are blank except one which is marked with an X. The child who receives the paper with the X is "It" but should be careful to conceal his or her role.

The children run, hop, skip, jump, or crawl around the play area looking at everyone's eyes. "It" winks at individuals as they move, trying not to bring attention to himself or herself. A person who is winked at must count to ten silently before becoming a "tree" with arms extended in the air, a "rock" curled up on the ground, or "grass" lying flat on the ground. Then he or she stays "frozen" until the game is over.

The game is over when everyone is frozen or when someone correctly accuses "It" of freezing others. If a child is falsely accused, the accuser is automatically frozen.

Lost in the Forest

Early elementary

Kids try to pass through the "forest" without being touched by any gently swaying "trees."

Choose five children to be the "forest." Space them across the room so that when their arms are spread out, their hands almost touch.

Members of the forest must keep their eyes closed and sway their arms from side to side. The other children must stand at a start line and then walk upright between the trees, trying to get to the other side of the forest without being touched. If a child is touched, he or she must freeze. One round consists of children going through the forest and coming back to the start line.

When a round is finished, the children who have been touched become part of the forest and are arranged in a second row. The second row of trees should be staggered behind the first row so that getting through the forest is even more challenging.

The game continues until all the children are trees.

Tiptoe Tag

Early elementary

Kids support one another in this small-group game of Tag.

Have kids form groups of four. Have each group form its own circle and hold hands. Everyone must stand on one foot and raise the other foot off the ground.

The object is to touch (*not* stomp) the tiptoes of the "down" foot of the others in the circle with your "up" foot. Anyone who stomps is immediately out of the game.

Once a foot is chosen as down, the same foot must remain down for the whole game. The up foot can't touch the floor. When a player's toes have been touched three times, he or she must place both feet on the ground but continue to hold hands with the others and encourage them.

Gates

All ages

Everyone must stay alert in this game of running action.

Have the children join together to form a circle. They should be able to touch the shoulder of each person standing next to them. Instruct the kids to stand with their arms crossed behind their backs. Choose two children to be runners. Each runner removes one shoe and places it on his or her head. Then the runners stand outside the circle about ten feet apart. When you say "go," the runners begin to chase each other clockwise around the circle.

After the runners have gone around the circle once, one runner may go through the "gates," or any two children standing together. Whenever a runner passes between two children in the circle, those children will bring up their arms, closing the gate so no runner can go through. Runners may go through any open gate to try to tag the other one. If a shoe falls, the runner must stop and replace it on his or her head before continuing. The game is over when one child catches the other or when one of the runners becomes closed inside the circle.

Play this game enough times for everyone to have a chance to be a runner.

PLAYMASTER'S POINTERS

Pick up the pace of this game by eliminating the shoe on the head of each runner.

Masking Tape Golf

BEST FOR Middle and upper elementary

Kids form a human golf course for this game of mini golf.

Make a lightweight ball about three or four inches in diameter by wadding up several sheets of paper and lightly wrapping the wad with masking tape. Have kids form two teams. Say: **We're going to be playing a game that's something like golf. But there are a few big differences: People's hands are going to be the "holes"; we'll use a ball made of paper and** tape; we'll play without clubs; and we'll play in teams instead of individually. Also, the holes will be *helping* the golfers get the ball in the hole.

Have one team form the course, spreading out at reasonable distances within the space you have. Let the other team begin by having the first person on the team toss the ball toward the first hole. Instruct the kids who are playing the part of the holes to do all they can, without moving their feet, to catch the ball. If the ball lands on the ground, have the next person on the team toss it toward the hole again. Keep rotating players, tossing from the first team until that team completes the course. Then have teams trade roles and play the game again.

Encourage all the kids to cheer each time a hole catches the ball. Don't bother keeping score; everyone is working together, so no one loses.

And It Was Very Good

BEST FOR Early or middle elementary

Kids revisit creation through items they find in their own backyard.

Begin by reading aloud Genesis 1:1, 6, 9-11, 14, 20, 24, 26, 31. Have children go outside and each find one thing that is small enough to bring inside. It must be something kids can pick up without killing any animals or bugs. For example, kids might bring blades of grass, leaves, stones, fallen sticks, dandelions, or pieces of litter. When everyone has found something, have kids come back inside.

Designate four different areas in your room, and number them 1 through 4. Then give the following instructions:

● **If you brought in something that is green and was recently living, move to area 1** (leaves, grass, flowers).

● **If you brought in something that was made by**

PLAYMASTER'S POINTERS

If there are things such as flowers around your meeting place that should not be disturbed, be sure kids know that.

humans, move to area 2 (paper, Popsicle stick, pop can).

● **If you brought in something that was alive but is now dead and is not green, move to area 3** (bug, tree branch, popcorn).

● **If you brought in something that was made by God but has never been living, move to area 4** (stone, dirt, sand).

Once kids have moved to their areas, have them discuss what characteristics each of their items have in common and why they chose what they did. Then have each group make up a fun story about the day God created the items they chose. Allow groups five minutes to develop their stories; then have each group share its story with the other kids.

Human Slingshots

 Middle to upper elementary

Kids must work together to hit the target in this fun partner game.

Have kids form pairs. Have a stack of recyclable paper ready for the kids to make small "stones." Designate a tree or another natural object to be a target.

Allow kids to stand wherever they want around the play area. To form a "sling," each pair must stand side by side and interlace the fingers of their closest hands. Before making a small stone from paper, each pair should practice moving their connected arms as one. Tell kids to think about how the band of a slingshot is pulled back and released to get an idea of how they should attempt to move their arms.

Each pair should then use its paper stone to load its human slingshot. Then pairs should take aim at the tree or other target. Each time a pair hits the target, the pair needs to take one step back. The kids will really enjoy perfecting their technique as they practice.

One great thing about this game is that all the pairs can play at the same time since their ammunition is harmless. Kids should retrieve the stones as soon as they land so they reuse them.

When kids are done playing the game, have them collect all the paper stones from the playing area; then congratulate each of your "slingers"!

Flamingo Tag

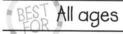 **BEST FOR** Middle to upper elementary

Players take on a one-foot challenge as they play this game of Circle Tag.

Have all the children stand in a circle. Choose one child to be "It." The rest of the players continue standing in the circle, but as soon as "It" begins making his or her way around the circle, all the players must stand on one foot and hold the other foot with their hands. "It" continues around the circle and will tag someone on the shoulder. That person will chase "It" and try to tag the player before he or she reaches the vacant place in the circle. Both players run with both legs. If the player tags "It," he or she becomes the new "It."

The players standing in the circle may switch feet at any time, but they must always keep one foot off the ground. If "It" sees a player standing with both feet on the ground, he or she may call out the player's name; then that player must immediately begin running in the same direction "It" is going, trying to tag "It" before he or she can snatch the player's space. "It" can also call, "It's raining!" Then the entire circle must raise the arm not holding the foot as though holding an umbrella. If any player loses his or her balance and drops a foot to the ground, "It" can call out that person's name to begin the chase.

Shadow Child

BEST FOR All ages

Identify classmates by their outlines in this modern adaptation of an ancient African game.

You'll need chalk or watercolor markers unless you have sand or soft dirt in a play area. Choose two children to stand outside the play area and not peek, or have children hold their hands over each other's eyes.

Meanwhile, the rest of the children should silently choose

another child who will lie down on the ground. Kids can work together to quickly trace that child's outline using the supplies available. As soon as the child's outline has been drawn, he or she should rejoin the group. They should all join hands and say the following rhyme:

Shadow, shadow on the ground,
Where, oh where is your body found?

The kids who were standing away from the group should come back and try to figure out whose body was traced to make the shadow child. These kids can ask up to two children to lie in the shadow space to see if the shadow fits. Then these kids can make one final guess if one of the people they've already chosen wasn't correct. If these kids are correct, they choose two new players to leave the area. If not, the shadow child is revealed and the guessers go back for another try.

QUIET QUESTERS

Quiet Questers will involve your kids in thoughtful and creative fun. Each of the games in this section can be played indoors—most in tight spots. You'll find games that encourage kids in a whole different kind of movement than relays and games of Tag. Your artistic and language-oriented kids will shine as they play games that are fun and challenging to them. These games are a blast in a different way from the rest of the games in this book, but shh! Kids will figure that out on their own!

Dark Valley

BEST FOR **Upper elementary**

Help kids understand that God is with them even in frightening situations or scary places.

This game is based on Psalm 23:4: "Even though I walk through the valley of the shadow of death, I will fear no evil, for you are with me." It can take place almost anywhere, but the church building is one of the best places of all. Get permission to use the church on a night when no one else will be around; then start the game by locking all the doors and turning out *all* the lights! Tell the kids that *no one* may exit the building during the game.

This game is similar to the old favorite Hide-and-Seek. However, in Dark Valley one person hides while all the others close their eyes and count to fifty. The person hiding tries to find a nook or cranny he or she can slip into and not be found.

When the others go looking, they must spread out. When a "seeker" finds the person who is hiding, the seeker slips into the hiding place, too. Everyone must remain quiet throughout this game to avoid giving away the hiding place and to add to the experience of being "alone."

Although the person who hides first may have some sense of the Psalm 23:4 experience, the player who is the last to find the hiding place will experience it even more. Imagine walking around in a darkened sanctuary, not seeing or hearing anyone else and knowing that somewhere a whole group of people is hiding and waiting for you!

When the last person finally finds the rest of the gang, everyone comes out and plays another round. The last seeker to find the others starts the next round by hiding.

PLAYMASTER'S POINTERS

Give the first person to hide the "point" of the lesson written on a slip of paper. Tell the person who's hiding to whisper this message to each person who joins him or her. You can use the message "The Lord is my shepherd" for a lesson on Psalm 23; "Perfect love drives out fear" for 1 John 4:18; or "My peace I give you" for a lesson about Jesus sending the Holy Spirit in John 14:27-31.

Wacky Stories

Middle or upper elementary

Involve kids in creative conversation while challenging them to think through the key ideas from various Bible stories.

On an index card, write five key words from a well-known Bible story or from a lesson you've recently covered with your class. The card should have five words that pertain to the same story. Make several cards that each refer to different stories so you have a deck filled with different options. Here are some examples:

> **Bible story:** Moses in the reeds
> **Key words:** basket, Nile, Pharaoh, baby, pitch
>
> **Bible story:** Jesus' birth
> **Key words:** hay, taxes, angels, census, inn
>
> **Bible story:** Jesus' resurrection
> **Key words:** stone, gardener, Mary, angels, cloths

Ask for a volunteer to go first. Have this player draw a card and make up a story—the wilder and more creative the better—using all five of the key words on the card. The goal is to "hide" the words in the story so none of the listeners can figure out which words were on the card.

Give one minute for the storyteller to complete the story. The storyteller must use *all* of the words to be successful.

When the storyteller is finished, let the audience try to guess what the five key words were. Each audience member may make one guess.

After all the audience members have guessed, reveal any remaining words. Write all five words on a chalkboard so everyone can see them. Have the audience and storyteller guess which Bible story was the common thread for all five words.

For more involvement, have your students work in teams to make up their own lists of five words.

PLAYMASTER'S POINTERS

If you have shy children, you can have the kids form teams and write out stories to read to other teams. This is a good way to have multi-age groups of children play together successfully. You can combine the imagination of younger children with the writing and reading abilities of older kids.

Dress Best

All ages

Can your kids detect subtle changes in their partners' appearances?

Have the students form pairs and sit down across from each other. Say: **For the next minute, I want you to look very carefully at what your partner is wearing. Then I will** turn off the lights. Turn away from each other, and change something about the way you're dressed. For example, you might put your shoes on the wrong feet or take off your socks and put your shoes back on. After you have made your change, wait until I turn the lights back on. Then face your partner again and see if you can tell what has changed.

Kids may have to stretch their imaginations to change their appearances. If someone is struggling, you might suggest one of the following changes:

● **Tuck in (or pull out) your shirt.**
● **Roll up the legs of your pants to make tiny cuffs.**
● **Roll your sleeves under.**
● **Untie your shoes or remove your shoelaces.**
● **Pull your socks straight up.**

Say: **Sometimes it's really hard to figure out a little change!** Affirm each child's effort.

Who Am I?

Upper elementary

This game gives kids a quiet indoor activity that turns their brains on to Bible facts and challenges their knowledge of Bible characters.

Who Am I? may be played with just about any size of group. Choose one player be "It" first. "It" picks a Bible character and tells the other players three things about this character without revealing the character's name. The catch is that only two of the three things can be true. One of the three statements must be false.

For example, if "It" is thinking of Paul, he or she might say the following:

● "This person wrote some of the Bible" (true);

● "This person was one of the twelve disciples" (false); and

● "This person could *not* walk on water" (true—he almost drowned when he was shipwrecked).

Each player asks "It" one question that can be answered with "yes" or "no." Then all of the players vote on which statement was not true.

After the vote, "It" reveals which statement was not true, and the other players take turns making guesses at who the Bible character really is.

Play this game until each child who wants to has had a turn.

I Love Jesus! Yes, I Do!

BEST FOR **Early elementary**

Help kids have fun while expressing their love for Jesus and others.

Say: To play this game, you need to repeat what I say exactly the way I say it. Ready? I love Jesus! Yes, I do! (I love Jesus! Yes, I do!) **Again, I love Jesus! Yes, I do!** (I love Jesus! Yes, I do!) **Did you know that Jesus commands us to love him with all of our bodies? In Matthew 22:37-38 Jesus says, "Love the Lord your God with all your heart** [point to your heart] **and with all your soul** [point to your entire body] **and with all your mind"** [point to your head]. **Jesus also says, "Love your neighbor as yourself." Who are some of your neighbors?** Allow time for answers. **Let's use the same rhythm we used before and express our love for our neighbors. I'll start, and you'll repeat after me. I love** [name of child]**! Yes, I do!** (I love [name of child]! **Yes, I do!**)

Change the rhythmic pattern of the chant. Here are some examples.

Get *really* creative using different musical patterns such as the one noted here.

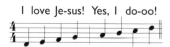

At this point, have the children create their own sentences such as "I love Mommy! Yes, I do," and have other children repeat after them. Suggest that kids use the names of people in the classroom and their families. Let kids get really creative.

Two on a Crayon

BEST FOR Early and middle elementary

Children cooperate to create a one-of-a-kind picture.

Say: **The Bible tells us that a true friend is closer than a brother or sister. Today we're going to practice being that kind of friend. Let's imagine for a minute how people would act if they were those kind of friends to each other.** Brainstorm with the children for a few minutes, and list ways people treat each other when they are very close friends. Kids may mention ideas such as "always kind," "there for each other," and "thoughtful of each other's needs and feelings."

Say: **Sometimes close friends even think alike. You will have a chance to see if you and a friend can think alike.** Have each child choose a partner. Give each pair one crayon and one piece of construction paper. Say: **You and your partner are going to make a picture together, with both of you holding the crayon and drawing and coloring together. You may not talk to each other while you work or before you begin. You can make any kind of picture you like.** Play some quiet music, if available, for three or four minutes; then gather children into a circle with partners sitting together. Go around the circle, asking partners to tell about their drawings. Then ask:

● **How did you feel about being asked not to talk to your partner?**

● **Did each partner share equally in drawing the picture? How could you tell?**

● **Which partner was the leader? How did you know?**

● **What did you learn about cooperation?**

Then have each person finish these statements with his or her partner:

- "I liked it when..."
- "I was glad when..."
- "I like our picture because..."

Silent Telephone

BEST FOR All ages

Kids pantomime clues to determine a familiar theme.

Have kids form two or more equal teams of no more than six members. Have teams line up facing one direction; then give the last person in each line a piece of paper with a word written on it (whisper the word for nonreaders). When ready, the person with the word taps the shoulder of the person in front of him or her and silently acts out the word. When the second person thinks he or she knows the word, he or she taps the shoulder of the third person and acts out the word.

The object of the game is to use three word clues to figure out a theme. Select easy words and send them in "clue trios": "ball," "bat," and "pitcher," for example. The team would then guess the theme "baseball" or "softball."

When the second person delivers the clue to the third person, initiate the next word in the series. Continue the process until the person at the front of the line has written down what he or she thinks each word is.

As soon as the front person knows all three words, the team huddles together and tries to figure out the theme. When the team thinks it knows the theme, it should send a reporter to verify the theme with you.

TRY THIS

With older kids, tell them they cannot repeat the motions that were given to them. Each person has to come up with a new idea to communicate the words.

Creative Kids

Upper elementary

Kids envision great endings from simple beginnings in this art-related game.

Have kids sit in a circle. Give each person a piece of paper and a pen or pencil. Then say: **We're going to make many group pictures using everyone's creativity, and we'll see what we come up with!** Have kids write their names on their papers and then each make one mark or squiggle. Each person should also think about what he or she imagines the finished drawing might look like. Then have kids pass the papers to their right and add some artistic details to the new papers. Remind kids that they are trying to make something out of all the lines. Keep passing until the pictures return to their original artists. The original artists can add a few finishing touches.

Have each artist explain what he or she had in mind with the first squiggle on his or her paper. Ask:

● **How is your finished piece similar to or different from your original idea?**

● **How is this experience like our lives?**

● **What do you think you can do about unexpected events in your life?**

Say: **We don't always know what's coming our way, and things don't always turn out the way we expect. But we can depend on God to use all those many differences for something good.**

Bible Alphabet Treasure Hunt

 Middle to upper elementary

Use this low-structure game to help your kids get into their Bibles.

Beginning with the letter A, have kids shout out words from the Bible that begin with each letter of the alphabet. For more difficult letters such as X, you can allow "ex" words.

Limit the kind of word the kids can list—for example, only Bible names or Bible places or books of the Bible.

The aim of this game is to make your way completely through the alphabet by finding a Bible word, phrase, or character that begins with every letter. Encourage students to delve deeper into their memories and their Bibles by probing for multiple responses to each letter. You might consider challenging older students to use only words they can *locate* in their Bibles!

Hey, Hey, Remember A?

 Upper elementary

Kids give clues about their understanding of key Bible principles as they play this word-smart game.

From a recent lesson, choose a theme word such as "faith," "fellowship," or "love." Or choose a Bible character's name. Boldly print each letter of the word or name down the left side of a piece of poster board or newsprint. Organize the students into groups of three or four, and assign each group one letter of the word. Instruct the groups to think of as many things as possible that begin with their letters and are related to the key word.

Specify a time limit for groups to complete their lists. Once the time limit is up, gather the students together.

Have each group share its findings, explaining how the words relate to the key word. Write the items mentioned with the corresponding letter on the poster board or newsprint. You can allow other class members to suggest other items that begin with that letter, or you can discuss some important related words that are not represented by a letter of the key word.

P Prison

A Athens
And Silas
Aquila

U Understand
Jews

L Lydia,
Liked travel

This is a great game to help you evaluate how well kids are understanding the implications of the key concepts they are learning during class time. You get not only the facts kids have learned, but also explanations of their thought processes as they file the concepts in their "mental notebooks."

Terrific Tales

BEST FOR Middle and upper elementary

Imagination rules as everyone's ideas are joined together to create a one-of-a-kind story.

Give each student paper and crayons or markers. Tell kids to draw something they think would be fun to tell a story about. After a couple of minutes, have kids explain what they put on their papers.

Have kids hold their papers and form a circle. Join the circle, holding your own paper, and say: **We're going to use what's on these papers to create a fun story. Here's how it will work. I'll begin the story by saying a sentence or two that involves what's on my paper. Then I'll call out a number between two and five. We'll count together as we pass each paper to the right the number of times I called out. Then the person next to me will say a sentence or two that adds to the story and will include something about what's on the paper he or she is holding. We'll continue until we get all the way around the circle, and the last person will end the story.**

If you have fewer than eight kids, you may want to go around the circle more than once for each story. If you have more than fourteen kids, you may want to form multiple circles.

Begin the story, call out a number, and lead children in counting to that number as they pass the papers to the right simultaneously. Continue as described, varying the number of times papers are passed. Be sensitive to kids who struggle with story lines, giving suggestions they could use before they get embarrassed.

Create as many stories as you have time for. If another adult is available, you might want to have that person write down the stories and copy them for kids to take home.

Handy Charades

BEST FOR Middle or upper elementary

Kids work together to portray familiar song titles using only their hands.

Have kids form groups of about four. Say: **We're going to play a little game called Handy Charades. In this game, each group will use only the group members' hands (wrist to fingertips) to try to help the rest of the group guess the song title that group has been assigned. You may form symbols, creatures, letters, or objects with your fingers or hands, but you may not use any other part of your body or say anything.** Give each group a slip of paper containing one of the following song titles, or add others you know your kids are familiar with:

- "Row, Row, Row Your Boat"
- "Twinkle, Twinkle, Little Star"
- "Jesus Loves Me"
- "Three Blind Mice"
- "Pop! Goes the Weasel"
- "Old MacDonald Had a Farm"
- "Jingle Bells"

Give each group about a minute to plan how they'll silently use their fingers to portray the song title to the rest of the group. Then have the first group begin. When the class guesses the correct song title, have another group present its song title using only its hands.

If a group seems to be struggling, take the kids aside, and give them suggestions for portraying the title.

If you have time, do a second round with new song titles. This time consider limiting the group to using only their fingers.

TRY THIS

Really creative groups might be challenged to use their bare feet instead of hands!

Follow On

BEST FOR All ages

Kids make beautiful rhythm patterns with this game that follows the same principle as the "wave."

Have the kids stand in a single-file line. Explain that the leader will make a movement, such as raising both hands over his or her head. The next person in line will follow, but the third person will keep his or her eyes on the second person and not perform the action until the second person has completed it. This process will continue down the line until every player has performed the action in turn.

Some other actions the leader might do are bending down on one knee, leaning far to the left or right, raising and lowering a leg to the side, putting hands on hips, or jumping straight up.

When your group has caught on to the strategy, try adding a musical background. It's fun to have one or two kids sit out to be the audience while the rest do the actions so the audience can see how beautiful this performance can be.

TRY THIS

For a discussion with your older children, this game can be a starting point for 1 Corinthians 11:1: "Follow my example, as I follow the example of Christ." Kids will quickly recognize the connection between the game and the Scripture!

Pass the Sound Around

BEST FOR All ages

This is a great game to play with a choir since it builds some of the same skills required for making beautiful music.

TRY THIS

Practice singing vowels with this game, assigning the vowel sound you want the kids to practice and allowing them to choose the pitch. Older kids can practice harmony using this strategy, with the first person initiating the pitch and holding it while the rest of the players add a harmonic tone.

Have the children lie on their backs in a circle on the floor with their heads together so they look like a flower. Choose one child to start. Then have all the children close their eyes so they're using only their hearing to play this game.

A selected child will make a sound. It can be a hummed note, a whistle, a click of the tongue, or any other sound a child can create. The next child to the right must imitate the sound to the best of his or her ability. Then the third child will make the sound. When everyone in the circle has made the sound, all the children can make the sound together and listen for unity. Then the second child in the circle can initiate another sound.

Continue until all the children have had a turn to start passing a sound.

Laws and Guffaws

BEST FOR Upper elementary

Challenge kids to discover what unwritten law is governing their game.

Choose two or three people to stand outside hearing distance of the rest of the group. The group must decide on a "law" they're going to observe in answering any question they may be asked. For example, the group decides that kids must pull their ears before answering, begin each answer with the word "the," or cover their mouths with their hands after each answer. Kids may be as creative as they want in establishing the law, but they must come to agreement within two minutes.

Have the "outsider" group come in and begin asking people in the first group questions about themselves. The outsiders can confer about what they notice in the answers. If the outsiders have not figured out the law by the time they've questioned each person in the group, reveal the law, and give the outsiders another turn. If the outsiders figure out the law, they each can choose a person to replace himself or herself.

Have the kids answer the questions as though they are a certain animal, Bible character, or object. For example, if the Bible character is King David, the question "What color is your hair?" might be answered, "I'm not sure, but my son got his hair caught in a tree one day!" If the person is a mother and the question is, "What color is your hair?" the answer might be, "It's brown when it's not covered with oatmeal!"

Animal-ization Celebration

 Early and middle elementary

Kids bring their animal dreams to life in this imaginative game.

Gather the children together in a circle. Ask them to close their eyes and think of an animal they've always dreamed of being. Have them imagine how that animal moves—how its eyes move, its head moves, its mouth moves, and finally how its whole body moves. Then have children think about how this animal moves when different things are happening—when it's chasing or being chased, when it's waking up or going to sleep, and when it sees a person in its space.

Have the children open their eyes, and teach them this rhyme:

Way back on that day of creation,
God gave cause for celebration
When he created me.
Can you guess who I might be?

Ask if one of the children is ready to act out the animal he or she has been thinking of. Have a child go inside the circle, and lead him or her to act out the small behaviors you have asked the children to imagine.

- **Show us how your eyes move.**
- **Show us how your mouth moves.**
- **Show us how you move when you're sleepy.**
- **Show us how you act when you're in danger!**

Ask the rest of the class to make some guesses about what animal the child *could* be acting out. Then let the child reveal which animal he or she was portraying. Encourage the children to celebrate the creation of that animal with cheering, clapping, and stomping. Then have children repeat the poem together, and allow another child to act out his or her animal.

Continue playing until each child who wants to has had a turn.

Body Lingo

BEST FOR Upper elementary

Who knows what the nose knows in this game that challenges kids to speak with all their body parts.

Say: **If I were to ask you to say "hello" to me without using any words, show me what you would do.** Pause for responses. **If I were to ask you to tell me that something tastes yummy without using any words, show me what you would do.** Pause. **How about if I asked you to tell me about the smell of a skunk without using words? Then what you would do? How about if I just asked you to say "yes" without words? Show me what that would look like.**

When kids nod their heads, explain that while they just said "yes" to you, if they had been in parts of the Middle East, they just would have said "no"!

Say: **Our body language says something because we all have learned and agreed that it says something.** Have the children form groups of four. Explain that each group's job is to come up with three gestures that communicate something their group feels is important. Then it will be their job to get the rest of the class to do something or respond in a certain way based on the gestures they develop.

Give each group between five and ten minutes to develop their gestures and practice them so that they all know what each one means. Then call the groups back together. Each group will get two minutes to try to influence others to respond to their gestures. If they succeed, the person who performs the correct action can become an honorary member of their group and help them influence others. At the end of three minutes, the group must use words to teach the other class members what their gestures mean.

Have each group take its turn. Ask:

- **What was hard about playing this game?**
- **When are some times you've felt it was hard to understand what someone else was saying or asking you to do?**
- **How did that make you feel?**
- **Can you think of some times Christians seem to have a different language than people around them understand?**
- **What can we do about that?**

Say: **We can all improve how well we communicate. It is one of the most fun challenges in our lives!**

Muk

BEST FOR All ages

Have fun playing this game based on one traditionally played by Eskimo children.

Say: **The word "muk" means silence. The goal of this game is for you to remain silent no matter happens.**

Have the children sit in a circle. Choose one person to be in the center of the circle. This person will point to someone, and the chosen person must say "muk" and then sit totally still without smiling while the person in the center does whatever he or she can to get the person to laugh. If the person doesn't respond to the antics, the person in the center may choose another child from the circle. This person must respond by saying, "Muk, muk" without laughing and then remain silent. Then the center person can try to make either of the children laugh.

If no one is laughing, the person in the center may choose a third child who will respond by saying, "Muk, muk, muk" and then fall into a similar silence. Chances are that by this time, one of the three will be laughing without much effort from the person in the center. Whoever laughs first replaces the person in the center, and play begins again.

Play until everyone has had a chance to be in the center or has been "muk."

Scripture Index

Group Publishing, Inc.
Attention: Product Development
P.O. Box 481
Loveland, CO 80539
Fax: (970) 669-1994

Evaluation for *Just-Add-Kids Games* for *Children's Ministry*

Please help Group Publishing, Inc., continue to provide innovative and useful resources for ministry. Please take a moment to fill out this evaluation and mail or fax it to us. Thanks!

● ● ●

1. As a whole, this book has been (circle one)

not very helpful   very helpful

1   2   3   4   5   6   7   8   9   10

2. The best things about this book:

3. Ways this book could be improved:

4. Things I will change because of this book:

5. Other books I'd like to see Group publish in the future:

6. Would you be interested in field-testing future Group products and giving us your feedback? If so, please fill in the information below:

Name _____

Street Address _____

City _____ State _____ Zip _____

Phone Number _____ Date _____

BRING THE BIBLE TO LIFE FOR YOUR 1ST- THROUGH 6TH-GRADERS...
WITH GROUP'S HANDS-ON BIBLE CURRICULUM™
Energize your kids with Active Learning!

Group's **Hands-On Bible Curriculum**™ will help you teach the Bible in a radical new way. It's based on Active Learning—the same teaching method Jesus used.

In each lesson, students will participate in exciting and memorable learning experiences using fascinating gadgets and gizmos you've not seen with any other curriculum. Your elementary students will discover biblical truths and remember what they learn because they're doing instead of just listening.

You'll save time and money, too!

While students are learning more, you'll be working less—simply follow the quick and easy instructions in the **Teacher Guide**. You'll get tons of material for an energy-packed 35- to 60-minute lesson. And, if you have extra time, there's an arsenal of Bonus Ideas and Time Stuffers to keep kids occupied—and learning! Plus, you'll SAVE BIG over other curriculum programs that require you to buy expensive separate student books—all student handouts in Group's **Hands-On Bible Curriculum** are photocopiable!

In addition to the easy-to-use **Teacher Guide**, you'll get all the essential teaching materials you need in a ready-to-use **Learning Lab**®. No more running from store to store hunting for lesson materials—all the active-learning tools you need to teach 13 exciting Bible lessons to any size class are provided for you in the **Learning Lab**.

Challenging topics each quarter keep your kids coming back!

Group's **Hands-On Bible Curriculum** covers topics that matter to your kids and teaches them the Bible with integrity. Switching topics every month keeps your 1st-through 6th-graders enthused and coming back for more. The full two-year program will help your kids...

- make God-pleasing decisions,
- recognize their God-given potential, and
- seek to grow as Christians.

Take the boredom out of Sunday school, children's church, and midweek meetings for your elementary students. Make your job easier and more rewarding with no-fail lessons that are ready in a flash. Order Group's **Hands-On Bible Curriculum** for your 1st-through 6th-graders today.

Hands-On Bible Curriculum is also available for
Toddlers & 2s, Preschool, and Pre-K and K!